GRADE 1

McGraw-Hill Education
Math

Second Edition

Mc
Graw
Hill
Education

New York   Chicago   San Francisco   Athens   London   Madrid

Mexico City   Milan   New Delhi   Singapore   Sydney   Toronto

1 2 3 4 5 6 7 8 9   LWI   22 21 20 19 18 17

ISBN   978-1-260-11683-0
MHID   1-260-11683-2

e-ISBN   978-1-260-11684-7
e-MHID   1-260-11684-0

McGraw-Hill Education products are available at special quantity discounts
to use as premiums and sales promotions or for use in corporate training
programs. To contact a representative, please visit the Contact Us pages at
www.mhprofessional.com.

McGraw-Hill Education thanks Wendy Hanks for her
invaluable contributions to this new edition.

Table of Contents

Table of Contents

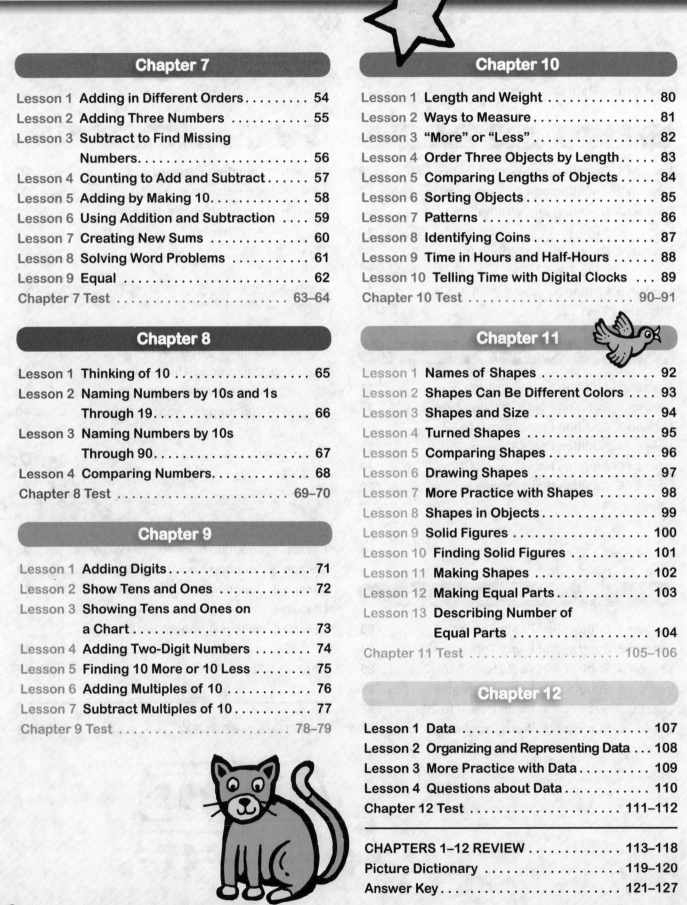

Welcome to McGraw-Hill Education's Math!

Parents, this book will help your child succeed in first grade mathematics. It will give your first grader:

- A head start in the summer before first grade
- Extra practice during the school year
- Helpful preparation for standardized mathematics exams

The book is aligned to Common Core State Standards. A chart beginning on the next page summarizes those standards and shows how each state that does not follow the Common Core differs from the Common Core standards. The chart also includes comparisons to Canadian standards.

If you live in a state that has adopted Common Core standards, you won't need the information in this table, although you may find its summary of Common Core standards helpful. Parents who live in Canada or states that have not adopted Common Core standards will find the table a useful tool and can be reassured that most of these regions have standards that are very similar to the Common Core. This book contains ample instruction and practice for students in any state or in Canada.

Students, this book will help you do well in mathematics. Its lessons explain math concepts and provide lots of interesting practice activities.

Open your book and look at the Table of Contents. It tells what topics are covered in each lesson. Work through the book at your own pace.

Each chapter ends with a Chapter Test. The results will show you what skills you have learned and what skills you may need to practice more. A final Review completes your work in this book and will show how you have done overall.

Take time to practice your math. Practicing will help you use and improve your math skills.

Good luck!

First Grade Math Standards

1st Grade U.S. Common Core Standards	Texas*	Virginia	Indiana	South Carolina
Represent and solve problems involving addition and subtraction.				
Understand and apply properties of operations and the relationship between addition and subtraction.		No related standards		
Add and subtract within 20.		Within 18	Fluently	
Work with addition and subtraction equations.		No related standards		
Extend the counting sequence (up to 120)	Also: backwards	Up to 100		
Understand place value.		Also: patterns	Also: ordinals, patterns	Also: patterns
Use place value understanding and properties of operations to add and subtract.		Also: ID fractions for 1/3, 1/2, 1/4		
Measure lengths indirectly and by iterating length units.		Also: volume, weight	Also: compare area, capacity, weight, temp.	
Tell and write time.	Also: ID coins, find value of coins	Also: ID coins, add coins to $1, read calendars	Also: Find value of coins	Also: ID coins
Represent and interpret data.				
Reason with shapes and their attributes.	Also: ID & name shapes	Also: ID & name shapes. Omits partitioning circles and rectangles into fractions		Also: ID & name 2D shapes

*Texas also has a section on personal financial literacy.

Minnesota	Oklahoma	Nebraska	Alaska	Canadian provinces
Omits properties of operations	No related standards			
	Within 10			
	Fewer standards			
	Up to 100			WNCP: up to 100
Also: patterns	Also: patterns	Also: patterns	Also: patterns	
Less focus on the properties of addition and subtraction				
Omits comparing lengths	Also: volume			ONT omits indirect measurement with 3rd object
Also: ID coins, add coins to $1	Also: ID coins, add coins to $1	Also: ID coins, add/subtract with coins	Also: calendars and ID coins	Only ONT
				WNCP omits
	Also: ID & name shapes			All omit defining attributes; Only ONT has fractions and composing 2D shapes

Counting and Writing from 0 to 5

You can count to find out how many.

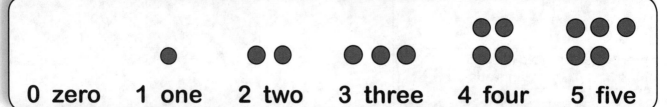

| 0 zero | 1 one | 2 two | 3 three | 4 four | 5 five |

Count

Tell how many. Circle the number.

1. 0   1   2   ③   4   5   2. 0   1   2   3   4   5

Tell how many. Write the number.

3. _____ 5

4. _____

5. _____

6. _____

7. _____

8. _____

Counting and Writing from 6 to 10

You can count to find out how many.

6 six   7 seven   8 eight   9 nine   10 ten

Count

Tell how many. Circle the number.

1   6   (7)   8   9   10

2   6   7   8   9   10

Tell how many. Write the number.

3   _8_

6   _____

4   _____

7   _____

5   _____

8   _____

Counting and Writing from 11 to 15

You can write numbers to tell how many.

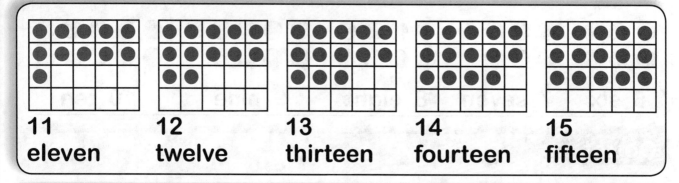

11 eleven   12 twelve   13 thirteen   14 fourteen   15 fifteen

Count

Tell how many. Circle the number.

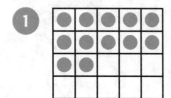

1. 11   (12)   13   14   15

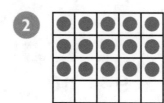

2. 11   12   13   14   15

Tell how many. Write the number.

3. 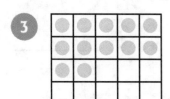   12

4. 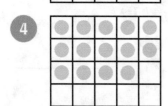   _____

5. 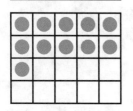   _____

6. 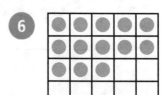   _____

7. 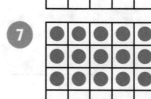   _____

8. 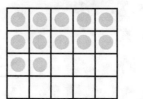   _____

Name _____

Counting and Writing from 16 to 20

You can write numbers to tell how many.

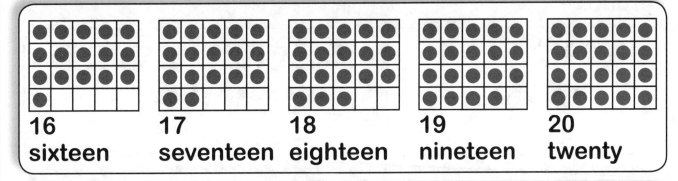

| 16 | 17 | 18 | 19 | 20 |
| sixteen | seventeen | eighteen | nineteen | twenty |

Count

Tell how many. Circle the number.

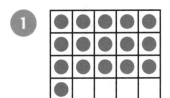

1. ⟨16⟩ 17 18 19 20   2.   16 17 18 19 20

Tell how many. Write the number.

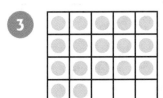

3.   _17_

6.   _____

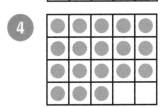

4.   _____

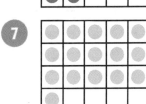

7.   _____

5.   _____

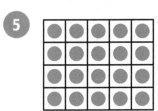

8.   _____

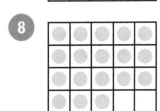

Name _____

Writing Numbers from 0 to 20

You can write numbers to tell how many things are in a group.

4

17

Count

Tell how many. Write the number. Use the cubes to help.

1 [cubes] _3_

5 [cube] _____

2 [cubes] _____

6 [cubes] _____

3  _____

7 [cubes] _____

4 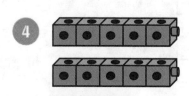 _____

8 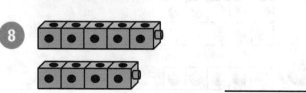 _____

Name _____

Count how many. Write the number.

1 🍊🍊🍊🍊 _____

6 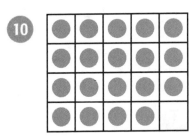 _____

2 🍎🍎🍎🍎🍎 🍎🍎🍎 _____

7 🍍🍍 _____

3 🍓🍓🍓🍓🍓 _____

8 _____

4 _____

9 _____

5 _____

10 _____

Name _____

Count how many. Write the number.

(11) 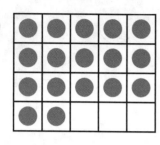 _____

(16) 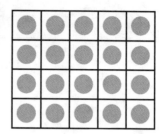 _____

(12)  _____

(17)  _____

(13) 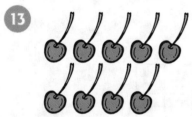 _____

(18) _____

(14) 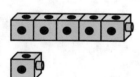 _____

(19)  _____

(15)  _____

(20) 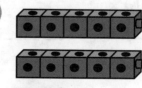 _____

Name _____

Lesson 1

Addition Facts Through 6

When you add, you group things together. You use a number sentence to show the sum.

Example

number sentence: 1   +   1   =   2

                        plus   equals   sum

Add

Write the sum.

1

$2 + 2 = \underline{\quad 4 \quad}$

4

$2 + 1 = \underline{\qquad}$

2

$1 + 4 = \underline{\qquad}$

5

$1 + 0 = \underline{\qquad}$

3

$3 + 3 = \underline{\qquad}$

6

$1 + 5 = \underline{\qquad}$

Chapter 2 • Lesson 1   **15**

Addition Facts Through 12

You can add by counting how many in each group.
Then count how many in all.

Example

Count each group.

○○○○○   ●●●

5   +   3

Count how many in all.

○○○○○●●●

5 + 3 = 8 in all

Add

Write the sum.

1 7 + 3 = __10__

4 8 + 4 = _____

2 4 + 5 = _____

5 6 + 1 = _____

3 5 + 6 = _____

6 4 + 4 = _____

Addition Facts from 0 to 12

Example

There are 3 circles. There are 5 squares. You can add to find how many shapes in all.

Count the circles.

3

Count the squares.

5

Start at 3. Count on 5.

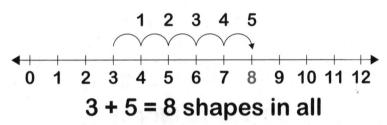

3 + 5 = 8 shapes in all

Add

Use the number line to find how many in all. Write the sum.

1. ▪▪ ▫▫▫

   2 + 3 = ___5___ shapes in all

2. ⬤⬤ ◯◯◯
   ⬤⬤ ◯◯

   4 + 5 = _____ shapes in all

3. 1 + 0 = _____

4. 5 + 7 = _____

5. 5 + 6 = _____

6. 6 + 1 = _____

7. 4 + 2 = _____

8. 2 + 1 = _____

Name _____

Addition Facts Through 20

Example

There are 8 red blocks. There are 7 blue blocks.
You can add to find how many blocks in all.

Count the red blocks.   **Count the blue blocks.**

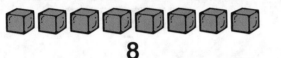

8   7

Start at 8. Count on 7.

1   2   3   4   5   6   7

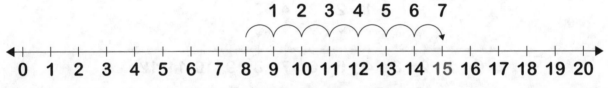

0   1   2   3   4   5   6   7   8   9   10   11   12   13   14   15   16   17   18   19   20

8 + 7 = 15 blocks

Add

Use the number line to find how many in all. Write the sum.

1. ●●●●● ○○○
    ●●●● ○○
    ●●

$10 + 5 =$ _15_ circles in all

2. ☆☆☆☆☆ ☆
    ☆☆☆☆☆
    ☆☆☆☆☆
    ☆☆☆

$18 + 1 =$ _____ stars in all

3. $6 + 5 =$ _____

4. $11 + 2 =$ _____

5. $13 + 7 =$ _____

6. $4 + 8 =$ _____

Name_____

Addition Facts from 0 to 20

You can add numbers to find the sum.

Example

Count the cats.   Count the dogs.

3   6

Find how many pets in all.
Start at 3. Count on 6.

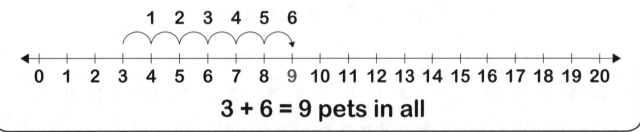

3 + 6 = 9 pets in all

Add

Use the number line to find how many in all. Write the sum.

1

3 + 3 = ___6___

2

9 + 2 = _____

3 5 + 10 = _____

4 1 + 1 = _____

5 13 + 7 = _____

6 14 + 0 = _____

Name _____

Addition Word Problems

You can add to solve word problems.

Example

| There are 3 red birds. | There are 2 blue birds. | How many birds in all? |

$$3 \qquad + \qquad 2 \qquad\qquad = \ ?$$

Start at 3. Count on 2.

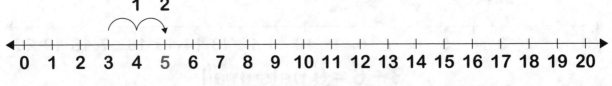

$$3 + 2 = 5 \text{ birds in all}$$

Solve

Add to solve each problem. Use the number line to help.

1 Sam has 7 ✏.
Ana has 2 ✏.
How many ✏ in all?

$$7 + 2 = \underline{\quad 9 \quad} ✏$$

2 There are 4 🍎 in a bowl.
There are 2 🍎 in a bag.
How many 🍎 in all?

$$4 + 2 = \underline{\qquad\quad} 🍎$$

3 Dan has 6 📖.
Lily has 8 📖.
How many 📖 are there?

$$6 + 8 = \underline{\qquad\quad} 📖$$

4 I see 6 dogs and 4 cats.
How many pets do I see?

$$6 + 4 = \underline{\qquad\quad} \text{pets}$$

Name _____

Add to find how many in all. Write the sum.
Use the number line to help.

0 1 2 3 4 5 6 7 8 9 10 11 12 13 14 15 16 17 18 19 20

1. $2 + 2 = $ _____ dogs

2. $2 + 1 = $ _____ cats

3. $3 + 2 = $ _____ cows

4. $7 + 4 = $ _____ horses

5. $4 + 4 = $ _____ pigs

6. $2 + 0 = $ _____ rabbits

7. $4 + 1 = $ _____ sheep

8. $3 + 9 = $ _____ fish

Name _____

Add. Write the sum.

9 5 + 5 = _____

10 2 + 7 = _____

11 1 + 1 = _____

12 6 + 3 = _____

13 1 + 11 = _____

14 3 + 5 = _____

15 14 + 5 = _____

16 8 + 5 = _____

17 9 + 8 = _____

18 0 + 14 = _____

Solve. Write the sum. Use the number line to help.

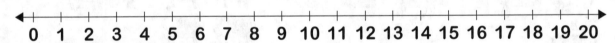

0 1 2 3 4 5 6 7 8 9 10 11 12 13 14 15 16 17 18 19 20

19 There are 5 pups playing.
There are 2 pups sleeping.
How many pups are there?

5 + 2 = _____ pups

20 Ed has 7 pens.
His mom has 5 pens.
How many do they have in all?

7 + 5 = _____ pens

Name _____

Subtraction Facts Through 6

When you subtract, you take away from a group. You use a number sentence to show the difference.

Example

5	–	2	=	3
	minus		equals	difference

Subtract

Subtract. Write your answer.

1

4 – 2 = ___2___

2

5 – 4 = _____

3

3 – 1 = _____

4

6 – 3 = _____

5

5 – 2 = _____

6

4 – 1 = _____

Name _____

Subtraction Facts Through 12

You can count back on a number line to subtract.

Example

12 – 5 = ?

Start at 12. Count back 5.

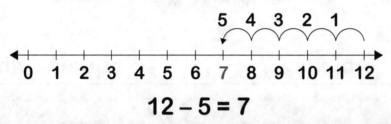

12 – 5 = 7

Subtract

Write the difference. Use the number line to help.

1 10 – 3 = __7__

6 10 – 7 = _____

2 11 – 5 = _____

7 7 – 2 = _____

3 8 – 6 = _____

8 11 – 10 = _____

4 12 – 1 = _____

9 9 – 3 = _____

5 10 – 5 = _____

10 12 – 8 = _____

Subtraction Facts from 0 to 12

You can count back on a number line to subtract.

Example

9 – 9 = ?

Start at 9. Count back 9.

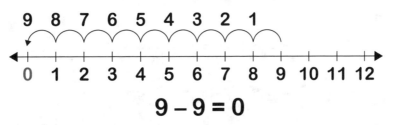

9 – 9 = 0

Subtract

Write the difference. Use the number line to help.

1 6 – 5 = ___1___

6 12 – 7 = _____

2 10 – 2 = _____

7 9 – 7 = _____

3 11 – 11 = _____

8 11 – 0 = _____

4 7 – 4 = _____

9 12 – 12 = _____

5 7 – 1 = _____

10 8 – 4 = _____

Name _____

Subtraction Facts Through 20

You can use objects to help you subtract.

Example

$$10 - 7 = ?$$

Start with 10. Count them. **Take away 7.** **Count how many are left.**

$$10 - 7 = 3$$

Subtract

Write the difference. Use objects to help.

1. $15 - 5 =$ __10__
2. $12 - 3 =$ __9__
3. $18 - 12 =$ _____
4. $14 - 13 =$ _____
5. $9 - 5 =$ _____

6. $6 - 4 =$ _____
7. $17 - 6 =$ _____
8. $20 - 4 =$ _____
9. $19 - 7 =$ _____
10. $8 - 1 =$ _____

Name _____

Subtraction Facts from 0 to 20

You can use small objects to help you subtract.

Example

Start with 8.
Count them.

$8 - 6 = ?$

Take away 6.

$8 - 6 = 2$

Count how many are left.

Subtract

Write the difference. Use objects to help.

1. $7 - 4 =$ ___3___

2. $13 - 3 =$ _____

3. $17 - 4 =$ _____

4. $11 - 4 =$ _____

5. $4 - 2 =$ _____

6. $9 - 0 =$ _____

7. $18 - 6 =$ _____

8. $20 - 15 =$ _____

9. $3 - 2 =$ _____

10. $19 - 8 =$ _____

11. $16 - 16 =$ _____

12. $14 - 6 =$ _____

Name _____

Subtraction Word Problems

Subtract to solve problems.

Example

There are 7 ducks.	4 ducks fly away.	How many ducks are left?

7   –   4   =   ?

Start at 7. Count back 4.

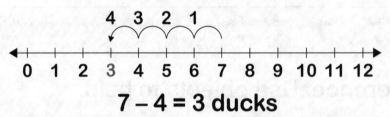

7 – 4 = 3 ducks

Solve

Subtract to solve the problems. Write the difference.

1 Sue has 8 🍎 in a bag. Sue gives 3 🍎 away. How many 🍎 does Sue have now?

8 – 3 = ___5___ apples

2 There are 17 🐎 in the field. 15 🐎 go into the barn. How many 🐎 are in the field now?

17 – 15 = _____ horses

Subtract. Write the difference. Use the number line to help.

$$\leftarrow 0\ 1\ 2\ 3\ 4\ 5\ 6\ 7\ 8\ 9\ 10\ 11\ 12\ 13\ 14\ 15\ 16\ 17\ 18\ 19\ 20 \rightarrow$$

1. ☐ ☒ ☒ ☒

   $4 - 3 =$ ___ 1

2. △ △ △ ☒ ☒

   $5 - 2 =$ ___ 3

3. ◯ ◯ ⊗ ⊗ ⊗ ⊗

   $6 - 4 =$ ___ 2

4. $11 - 7 =$ _____
5. $9 - 6 =$ _____
6. $12 - 6 =$ _____
7. $10 - 2 =$ _____
8. $8 - 1 =$ _____
9. $3 - 2 =$ _____
10. $10 - 10 =$ _____
11. $11 - 6 =$ _____

Subtract. Write the difference. Use small objects to help.

12. $7 - 3 =$ ___ 4
13. $16 - 5 =$ _____
14. $19 - 9 =$ _____
15. $14 - 6 =$ _____
16. $20 - 17 =$ _____
17. $15 - 15 =$ _____
18. $6 - 0 =$ _____
19. $12 - 7 =$ _____

Name _____

Solve the problems. Write the difference. Use the number line to help.

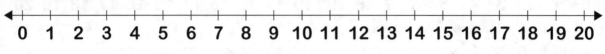

0 1 2 3 4 5 6 7 8 9 10 11 12 13 14 15 16 17 18 19 20

20 Carlos has 19 ✏.
Carlos gives 5 ✏ to Tom.
How many ✏ does
Carlos have now?

19 – 5 = _____ ✏

21 Tina has 18 ⊚.
Tina gives 2 ⊚ to Dad.
How many ⊚ does
Tina have left?

18 – 2 = _____ ⊚

22 A pet store has 20 🐟.
A man buys 7 🐟.
How many 🐟 are left?

20 – 7 = _____ 🐟

23 A bag has 19 🍬.
11 🍬 fall out.
How many 🍬 are in
the bag now?

19 – 11 = _____ 🍬

24 Ms. Lee has 13 ⭐.
She gives away 8 ⭐.
How many ⭐ does
she have left?

13 – 8 = _____ ⭐

25 7 dogs are in the park.
4 dogs go home.
How many dogs are in
the park now?

7 – 4 = _____ 🐕

26 Kay sees 10 ants.
5 ants go away.
How many ants are
left?

10 – 5 = _____ ants

Counting Forward

You can start counting with any number.

0	zero		11	eleven
1	one		12	twelve
2	two		13	thirteen
3	three		14	fourteen
4	four		15	fifteen
5	five		16	sixteen
6	six		17	seventeen
7	seven		18	eighteen
8	eight		19	nineteen
9	nine		20	twenty
10	ten			

Start with 6. Count to 10.

6 7 8 9 10

Count

Write the numbers.

1. 0 1 _2_ _3_ _4_

2. 4 5 ___ ___ ___

3. 6 7 ___ ___ ___

4. 14 15 ___ ___ ___

5. 11 12 ___ ___ ___

6. 8 9 ___ ___ ___

7. 16 17 ___ ___ ___

8. 9 10 ___ ___ ___

Name _____

Counting from 0 to 50

You can count from 0 to 50.

			0						
1	2	3	4	5	6	7	8	9	10
11	12	13	14	15	16	17	18	19	20
21	22	23	24	25	26	27	28	29	30
31	32	33	34	35	36	37	38	39	40
41	42	43	44	45	46	47	48	49	50

Count

Write the missing numbers. Then count aloud.

			0						
1	2	3	4	5		7		9	
	12		14	15		17	18		20
21				25	26	27		29	30
	32	33		35		37	38	39	
41	42			45	46	47			50

Name _____

Counting Forward from Any Number

You can start counting with any number.

Example

Start with 14. Count to 18.

14   15   16   17   18

Count

Write the numbers.

1. 6 7 _8_ _9_ _10_

6. 18 19 ___ ___ ___

2. 22 23 ___ ___ ___

7. 43 44 ___ ___ ___

3. 0 1 ___ ___ ___

8. 17 18 ___ ___ ___

4. Start with 2.

___ ___ ___ ___

9. Start with 25.

___ ___ ___ ___

5. Start with 33.

___ ___ ___ ___

10. Start with 47.

___ ___ ___ ___

Name _____

Tell what number comes next. Write the number.

1 0 _____   **5** 15 _____

2 5 _____   **6** 18 _____

3 9 _____   **7** 7 _____

4 3 _____   **8** 11 _____

9 ## Write the missing numbers.

0

	2	3	4			7		9	10
11		13				17	18	19	20
21	22		24	25	26	27		29	
	32	33		35	36	37			40
41	42		44	45			48	49	

Count. Write the numbers.

10 0 1 ___ ___ ___ ___

11 13 14 ___ ___ ___ ___

12 34 35 ___ ___ ___ ___

13 27 28 ___ ___ ___ ___

14 39 40 ___ ___ ___ ___

15 18 19 ___ ___ ___ ___

16 6 7 ___ ___ ___ ___

17 45 46 ___ ___ ___ ___

18 Start with 7.

___ ___ ___ ___

19 Start with 19.

___ ___ ___ ___

20 Start with 30.

___ ___ ___ ___

21 Start with 21.

___ ___ ___ ___

22 Start with 42.

___ ___ ___ ___

23 Start with 16.

___ ___ ___ ___

24 Start with 47.

___ ___ ___ ___

25 Start with 3.

___ ___ ___ ___

Name _____

Counting from 50 to 75

You can count past 50. You start at 50.
Then you count on.

50	fifty	**60**	sixty	**70**	seventy
51	fifty-one	**61**	sixty-one	**71**	seventy-one
52	fifty-two	**62**	sixty-two	**72**	seventy-two
53	fifty-three	**63**	sixty-three	**73**	seventy-three
54	fifty-four	**64**	sixty-four	**74**	seventy-four
55	fifty-five	**65**	sixty-five	**75**	seventy-five
56	fifty-six	**66**	sixty-six		
57	fifty-seven	**67**	sixty-seven		
58	fifty-eight	**68**	sixty-eight		
59	fifty-nine	**69**	sixty-nine		

Count

Read the number shown. Count on. Write the numbers.

① 50 _51_ _52_ _53_

② 54 ____ ____ ____

③ 61 ____ ____ ____

④ 70 ____ ____ ____

⑤ 53 ____ ____ ____

⑥ 58 ____ ____ ____

⑦ 66 ____ ____ ____

⑧ 72 ____ ____ ____

Counting from 76 to 100

You can count past 75. You can start at 76.
Then you count on.

76	seventy-six	86	eighty-six	96	ninety-six
77	seventy-seven	87	eighty-seven	97	ninety-seven
78	seventy-eight	88	eighty-eight	98	ninety-eight
79	seventy-nine	89	eighty-nine	99	ninety-nine
80	eighty	90	ninety	100	one hundred
81	eighty-one	91	ninety-one		
82	eighty-two	92	ninety-two		
83	eighty-three	93	ninety-three		
84	eighty-four	94	ninety-four		
85	eighty-five	95	ninety-five		

Count

Read the number shown. Count on. Write the numbers.

1. 76 _77_ _78_ _79_

2. 82 ____ ____ ____

3. 97 ____ ____ ____

4. 78 ____ ____ ____

5. 90 ____ ____ ____

6. 77 ____ ____ ____

7. 88 ____ ____ ____

8. 94 ____ ____ ____

Counting to 100 by 10s
You can count by 10s.

Example

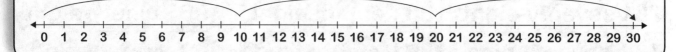

| 0 | 10 | 20 | 30 | 40 | 50 | 60 | 70 | 80 | 90 | 100 |

Count

Count by 10s aloud. Write the missing numbers.

1 0 __10__ __20__ 30

5 40 _____ _____ _____

2 50 60 _____ _____

6 60 70 _____ _____ _____

3 10 20 _____ _____

7 30 40 ___ 60 ___ ___

4 70 80 _____ _____

8 20 ___ ___ 50 ___

Name _____

Writing Numbers to 100

You can count to 100. You can write the numbers.

Count

Begin with 50. Complete the chart. Write the missing numbers.

1	2	3	4	5	6	7	8	9	10
11	12	13	14	15	16	17	18	19	20
21	22	23	24	25	26	27	28	29	30
31	32	33	34	35	36	37	38	39	40
41	42	43	44	45	46	47	48	49	50
51									

Name _____

Counting Forward to 100

You can count from 0 to 100. Start with any number. Then you count on.

Example

Start with 0.

0   1   2   3   4   5   6   7   8   9   10

Start with 52.

52   53   54   55   56   57   58   59   60   61   62

Count

Count aloud. Write the missing numbers.

1 1 2 3 __4__ __5__ __6__ 7 8 __9__

2 76 77 _____ 79 _____ _____ 82 _____ 84

3 91 92 _____ 94 _____ 96 97 _____ _____

4 50 _____ 52 _____ 54 _____ 56 _____ 58

5 82 _____ 84 _____ _____ 87 _____ 89 90

6 67 68 69 _____ _____ _____ _____ 74 75

7 17 18 _____ _____ 21 22 _____ 24 _____

8 33 _____ _____ 36 _____ 38 39 _____ 41

Name _____

1 ## Complete the chart. Write the missing numbers.

1	2		4	5	6	7		9	10
11	12	13	14	15		17	18		20
21		23	24		26	27	28	29	30
	32	33	34	35	36		38	39	40
41	42	43	44	45	46	47	48		
51		53		55	56	57	58	59	60
61	62	63	64	65	66	67		69	
	72	73	74		76	77	78	79	80
81	82		84	85		87	88	89	90
91	92	93		95	96		98	99	100

Count on. Write the missing numbers.

2 53 54 ____ ____ ____

3 60 61 ____ ____ ____

4 56 57 ____ ____ ____

5 69 70 ____ ____ ____

6 71 72 ____ ____ ____

7 79 80 ____ ____ ____

8 96 97 ____ ____ ____

9 77 78 ____ ____ ____

10 87 88 ____ ____ ____

11 89 90 ____ ____ ____

Name _____

Count by 10s. Write the missing numbers.

(12) 10 20 ____ ____ ____

(14) 30 40 ____ ____ ____

(13) 50 60 ____ ____ ____

(15) 60 70 ____ ____ ____

Count. Write the missing numbers.

(16) 50 ____ ____ 53

(21) 33 34 ____ 36 ____

(17) 85 ____ ____ ____

(22) 67 68 ____ ____

(18) 41 ____ 43 ____

(23) 80 ____ 82 ____

(19) 39 40 ____ ____

(24) 91 ____ ____ ____

(20) 96 97 ____ ____

(25) 17 ____ ____ 20

Counting from 100 to 120 by 1s

You can say and write numbers as you count.

100	one hundred	111	one hundred eleven
101	one hundred one	112	one hundred twelve
102	one hundred two	113	one hundred thirteen
103	one hundred three	114	one hundred fourteen
104	one hundred four	115	one hundred fifteen
105	one hundred five	116	one hundred sixteen
106	one hundred six	117	one hundred seventeen
107	one hundred seven	118	one hundred eighteen
108	one hundred eight	119	one hundred nineteen
109	one hundred nine	120	one hundred twenty
110	one hundred ten		

Count

Write the missing numbers.

1 Count from 100 to 103.

100 _101_ _102_ _103_

4 Count from 112 to 114.

_____ _____ _____

2 Count from 106 to 108.

_____ _____ _____

5 Count from 105 to 107.

_____ _____ _____

3 Count from 111 to 113.

_____ _____ _____

6 Count from 102 to 104.

_____ _____ _____

Name _____

Counting from 0 to 120 by 10s

You can count to 120 by 10s.

0	zero		70	seventy
10	ten		80	eighty
20	twenty		90	ninety
30	thirty		100	one hundred
40	forty		110	one hundred ten
50	fifty		120	one hundred twenty
60	sixty			

Count

Count by tens out loud. Write the missing numbers.

1 Count from 10 to 40 by 10s.

10 20 __30__ __40__

4 Count from 80 to 110 by 10s.

____ ____ ____ ____

2 Count from 80 to 110 by 10s.

80 90 ____ ____

5 Count from 0 to 30 by 10s.

____ ____ ____ ____

3 Count from 20 to 50 by 10s.

____ ____ ____ ____

6 Count from 50 to 80 by 10s.

____ ____ ____ ____

Counting from 0 to 100 by 5s

You can count by 5s.

0	zero	55	fifty-five
5	five	60	sixty
10	ten	65	sixty-five
15	fifteen	70	seventy
20	twenty	75	seventy-five
25	twenty-five	80	eighty
30	thirty	85	eighty-five
35	thirty-five	90	ninety
40	forty	95	ninety-five
45	forty-five	100	one hundred
50	fifty		

Count

Count by 5s. Write the numbers.

1 Count from 5 to 20 by 5s.

5 10 _15_ _20_

4 Count from 35 to 50 by 5s.

___ ___ ___ ___

2 Count from 30 to 45 by 5s.

30 35 _____ _____

5 Count from 60 to 75 by 5s.

___ ___ ___ ___

3 Count from 55 to 70 by 5s.

55 60 _____ _____

6 Count from 80 to 95 by 5s.

___ ___ ___ ___

Name _____

Counting by 1s, 5s, and 10s

You can count by 1s, 5s, or 10s.

Example

Count by 1s.	14, 15, 16, 17, 18, 19, 20, 21, 22, 23, 24
Count by 5s.	0, 5, 10, 15, 20, 25, 30, 35, 40, 45, 50, 55, 60, 65, 70, 75, 80, 85, 90, 95, 100, 105, 110, 115, 120
Count by 10s.	0, 10, 20, 30, 40, 50, 60, 70, 80, 90, 100, 110, 120

Count

Count out loud. Write the missing numbers.

1 Count by 1s.

38 39 _40_ _41_ _42_

2 Count by 5s.

85 90 ____ ____ ____

3 Count by 1s.

106 107 ____ ____ ____

4 Count by 5s.

25 30 ____ ____ ____

5 Count by 10s.

40 50 ____ ____ ____

6 Count by 10s.

80 90 ____ ____ ____

Writing Numbers to 120 by 5s and 10s

You can count by 5s and 10s. You can write the numbers that you count.

Example

You can write numbers by 5s.

0 5 10 15 20 25 30

You can write numbers by 10s.

0 10 20 30 40

Count

Count by 5s. Write the missing numbers.

0	5	10	15		25
	35				55
	65		75		
90		100		110	115
120					

Count by 10s. Write the missing numbers.

0	10	20			50
	70		90		110
120					

Name _____

Count on. Write the missing numbers.
Count by 1s. Write the missing numbers.

1 103 104 ____ ____ ____   **5** 56 57 ____ ____ ____

2 106 107 ____ ____ ____   **6** 67 68 ____ ____ ____

3 114 115 ____ ____ ____   **7** 97 98 ____ ____ ____

4 41 42 ____ ____ ____   **8** 75 76 ____ ____ ____

Count by 10s. Write the missing numbers.

9 0 10 ____ ____ ____   **13** 70 80 ____ ____ ____

10 80 90 ____ ____ ____   **14** 20 30 ____ ____ ____

11 50 60 ____ ____ ____   **15** 30 40 ____ ____ ____

12 40 50 ____ ____ ____   **16** 60 70 ____ ____ ____

Count by 5s. Write the missing number.

17 25 30 ____ ____ ____

21 80 85 ____ ____ ____

18 10 15 ____ ____ ____

22 35 40 ____ ____ ____

19 65 70 ____ ____ ____

23 100 105 ____ ____

20 0 5 ____ ____ ____

24 15 20 ____ ____ ____

25 Count by 5s. Write the missing numbers.

0		10	15	20	
30	35	40		50	55
	65	70	75		85
90		100	105	110	
120					

26 Count by 10s. Write the missing numbers.

0		20	30		50
	70	80		100	
120					

Name _____

Tell how many. Write the number.

1  _____

2  _____

3 _____

4 _____

5 _____

6  _____

7  _____

8  _____

9 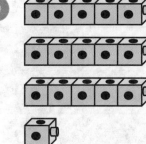 _____

10 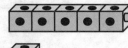 _____

Add to find out how many. Write the sum.
Use the number line to help.

0 1 2 3 4 5 6 7 8 9 10 11 12 13 14 15 16 17 18 19 20

11
3 + 2 = _____ oranges

13
1 + 5 = _____ apples

12
3 + 3 = _____ lemons

14
2 + 0 = _____ cherries

Add. Write the sum.

15 2 + 1 = _____

19 9 + 2 = _____

16 5 + 3 = _____

20 8 + 4 = _____

17 6 + 7 = _____

21 7 + 13 = _____

18 4 + 6 = _____

22 1 + 19 = _____

Name _____

Subtract. Write the difference.
Use the number line to help.

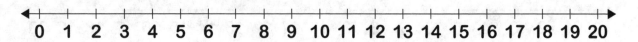

23 6 − 1 = _____

29 5 − 3 = _____

24 3 − 2 = _____

30 4 − 3 = _____

25 4 − 3 = _____

31 19 − 11 = _____

26 13 − 0 = _____

32 15 − 8 = _____

27 12 − 5 = _____

33 6 − 4 = _____

28 8 − 8 = _____

34 17 − 0 = _____

Count by 1s, 5s, or 10s. Write the missing numbers.

(35) 5 6 7 _____ _____ _____ _____ 12

(36) 65 70 _____ _____ 85 _____ _____

(37) 10 20 _____ 40 _____ _____ _____

(38) 25 30 _____ _____ _____ _____ 55

Solve. Write the sum or difference.

(39) Elsa has 4 🐟.
Nate has 5 🐟.
How many fish
in all?

4 + 5 = _____ fish

(41) There are 19 🐦.
3 🐦 fly away.
How many birds are left?

19 − 3 = _____ birds

(40) There are 8 🚗.
2 🚗 leave.
How many cars are left?

8 − 2 = _____ cars

(42) There are 7 red blocks
and 7 green blocks.
How many blocks
in all?

7 + 7 = _____ blocks

Name _____

Adding in Different Orders

You can add numbers in different orders. The sum will be the same.

Examples

$$4 + 2 = 6$$ $$2 + 4 = 6$$

You can add zero to any number. The sum is always the number.

$$0 + 4 = 4$$

Add

Write the sum.

1. $3 + 1 = \underline{4}$

   $1 + 3 = \underline{4}$

2. $4 + 3 = \underline{}$

   $3 + 4 = \underline{}$

3. $0 + 5 = \underline{}$

4. $6 + 0 = \underline{}$

5. $18 + 0 = \underline{}$

6. $0 + 19 = \underline{}$

Name _____

Adding Three Numbers

You can add three numbers. You can group the numbers in any way. The sum will be the same.

Example

$$2 + 3 + 4 =$$

Group two numbers. Add them.
Add their sum to the third number.

$$(2 + 3) + 4 = 9 \quad \text{or} \quad 2 + (3 + 4) = 9$$

$$5 \qquad\qquad 7$$

Add

Write the sum.

1. $(2 + 1) + 4 = \underline{7}$

   $2 + (1 + 4) = \underline{7}$

2. $(5 + 3) + 1 = \underline{}$

   $5 + (3 + 1) = \underline{}$

3. $(2 + 4) + 2 = \underline{}$

   $2 + (4 + 2) = \underline{}$

4. $(1 + 5) + 7 = \underline{}$

   $1 + (5 + 7) = \underline{}$

Name _____

Subtract to Find Missing Numbers

You can find a missing addend.

Example

A number is missing.

$$7 + \boxed{?} = 11$$

You can subtract the known addend to find the missing part.

$$11 - 7 = \boxed{4}$$

Solve

Read the number sentences. Write the missing number.

1 $5 + \boxed{?} = 6$

$6 - 5 = \underline{\quad 1 \quad}$

$5 + \underline{\quad 1 \quad} = 6$

2 $2 + \boxed{?} = 4$

$4 - 2 = \underline{\qquad}$

$2 + \underline{\qquad} = 4$

3 $9 + \boxed{?} = 18$

$18 - 9 = \underline{\qquad}$

$9 + \underline{\qquad} = 18$

4 $4 + \boxed{?} = 7$

$7 - 4 = \underline{\qquad}$

$4 + \underline{\qquad} = 7$

Counting to Add and Subtract

You can count on to add.

You can count back to subtract.

Examples

When you add 2, you can count on 2.

$$6 + 2 =$$

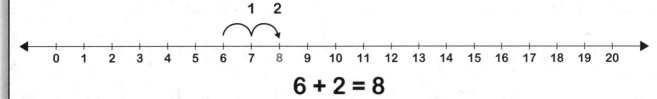

$$6 + 2 = 8$$

When you subtract 2, you can count back 2.

$$5 - 2 =$$

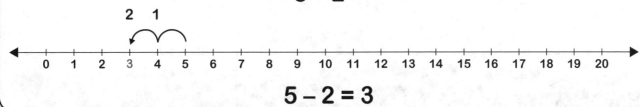

$$5 - 2 = 3$$

Add or Subtract

Count on to add. Count back to subtract. Write the sum or difference.

1. $4 + 5 =$ _9_

2. $15 - 4 =$ _____

3. $12 + 6 =$ _____

4. $11 - 5 =$ _____

5. $9 + 9 =$ _____

6. $7 - 1 =$ _____

7. $8 + 6 =$ _____

8. $19 - 14 =$ _____

Adding by Making 10

Making 10 can help you add.

Examples

Draw counters to show the problem.

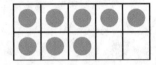 8

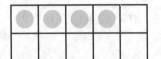 + 4

Then move counters to make 10.

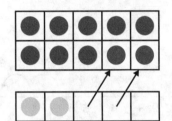 10

+ 2

The answers are the same.

$$10 + 2 = 12$$
$$8 + 4 = 12$$

Solve

Draw circles to make 10. Then write your answers.

1 7 + 5 = ?

 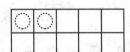

10 + 2 = _12_

so 7 + 5 = _12_

2 9 + 7 = ?

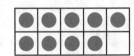 

10 + 6 = _____

so 9 + 7 = _____

Using Addition and Subtraction

When you know an addition fact, you also know a subtraction fact.

Example

This shows both addition and subtraction.

11 whole	
4 part	7 part

4 + 7 = 11
part part whole

7 + 4 = 11
part part whole

11 – 7 = 4
whole part part

11 – 4 = 7
whole part part

You add the parts to get the whole.

You subtract one part from the whole to get the other part.

Solve

Look at the chart. Write an addition sentence. Write a subtraction sentence.

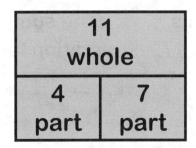

6 + 1 = 7

7 – 1 = 6

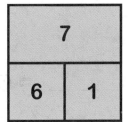

_____ + _____ = _____

_____ – _____ = _____

Name _____

Creating New Sums

Different numbers add up to the same sum.

This can help you add.

Examples

$9 + 8 = 17$	$10 + 7 = 17$	$11 + 6 = 17$
The sum of this addition fact is 17.	The sum of this addition fact is 17.	The sum of this addition fact is 17.

Solve

Look at the math fact. Write another fact with the same sum.

1 $12 + 3 = 15$

_10_ + _5_ = 15

2 $5 + 3 = 8$

_____ + _____ = 8

3 $9 + 4 = 13$

_____ + _____ = 13

4 $6 + 5 = 11$

_____ + _____ = 11

5 $7 + 3 = 10$

_____ + _____ = 10

6 $5 + 0 = 5$

_____ + _____ = 5

7 $4 + 2 = 6$

_____ + _____ = 6

8 $8 + 1 = 9$

_____ + _____ = 9

Solving Word Problems

Examples

Yuki draws 4 blue birds.	David draws 7 red birds.	How many birds did they draw in all?
4	+ 7	= ?

You can use objects to help you add or subtract. Here we count pennies.

Count 3 pennies.	Then count 2 more pennies.	How many pennies do you have? Count them.

There are 5 pennies.

Solve

Add or subtract to solve. Write the sum or difference. Use objects to help.

1 There are 14 bees.

5 bees fly away.

How many bees are left?

14 – 5 = ___9___

2 Ella draws 4 stars.

She draws 2 more stars.

How many stars does Ella draw?

4 + 2 = _____

Equal

Equal means to have the same amount or value.

Examples

These numbers are equal.	These number sentences show equal amounts.
$4 = 4$	$1 + 2 = 3$
$62 = 62$	$5 - 1 = 2 + 2$

An equal sign (=) tells that amounts are the same.

Identify

Look at each number. Write an equal number.

① $6 =$ _____ 6

③ $103 =$ _____

② $23 =$ _____ 23

④ $82 =$ _____

Look at each set of numbers. Write = if they are equal.
Write **not** = if they are not equal.

⑤ 25 _____ 32

⑦ $4 + 3$ _____ 7

⑥ 79 _____ 79

⑧ $2 + 6$ _____ $4 + 4$

Read the number sentences. Write the sums.

1 $5 + 7 =$ _____

$7 + 5 =$ _____

2 $12 + 6 =$ _____

$6 + 12 =$ _____

3 $0 + 8 =$ _____

4 $0 + 4 =$ _____

5 $5 + 1 + 2 =$ _____

6 $3 + 6 + 4 =$ _____

Read the problems. Write the missing number.

7 $5 + \boxed{?} = 9$

$9 - 5 =$ _____

$5 +$ _____ $= 9$

8 $5 + \boxed{?} = 18$

$18 - 5 =$ _____

$5 +$ _____ $= 18$

Look at each addition sentence. Write another fact with the same sum.

9 $9 + 2 = 11$

_____ $+$ _____ $= 11$

10 $3 + 4 = 7$

_____ $+$ _____ $= 7$

Look at each set of numbers. Write = if they are equal.
Write not = if they are not equal.

11 17 _____ 17

12 35 _____ $30 + 5$

13 $8 + 3$ _____ $12 + 5$

14 $9 - 3$ _____ $4 + 2$

Draw circles to make 10. Then write your answers.

15 8 + 5 = ?

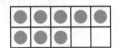

10 + 3 = _____

so 8 + 5 = _____

16 9 + 6 = ?

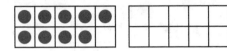

10 + 5 = _____

so 9 + 6 = _____

Count on to add. Count back to subtract.

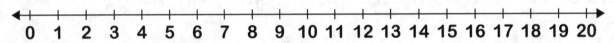

0 1 2 3 4 5 6 7 8 9 10 11 12 13 14 15 16 17 18 19 20

17 4 + 7 = _____

18 18 – 12 = _____

Look at the chart. Write an addition sentence. Then write a subtraction sentence.

6	
2	4

19 _____ + _____ = _____   **20** _____ – _____ = _____

Add or subtract to solve. Write the sum or difference. Use objects to help.

21 6  play.

2  sleep.

How many are there?

6 + 2 = _____

22 Ben has 13 .

He gives 6 to Sara.

How many does Ben have now?

13 – 6 = _____

Name _____

Thinking of 10

Examples

10 ones are equal to 1 ten

30 ones are equal to 3 tens.

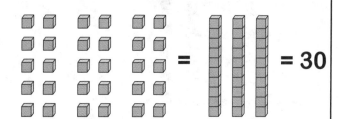

10 ones = 1 ten

30 ones = 3 tens

Count

Count the ones. Write how many ones. Write how many tens.

<u>30</u> ones

So there are __3__ tens.

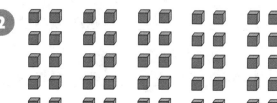

_____ ones

So there are _____ tens.

Naming Numbers by 10s and 1s Through 19

You can name numbers by tens and ones.

Examples

1 ten + 5 ones = 15

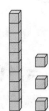

1 ten + 3 ones = 13

Solve

Use objects to show a number. Then write the number as a ten and ones.

1. 15 is ___1___ ten and ___5___ ones.

2. 14 is _____ ten and _____ ones.

3. 18 is _____ ten and _____ ones.

4. 12 is _____ ten and _____ ones.

5. 16 is _____ ten and _____ ones.

6. 19 is _____ ten and _____ ones.

7. 17 is _____ ten and _____ ones.

8. 13 is _____ ten and _____ ones.

Name _____

Naming Numbers by 10s Through 90

You can use tens to make numbers.

Example

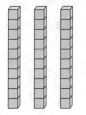

3 tens

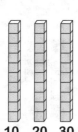

10 20 30

Count by 10s to find how many ones.

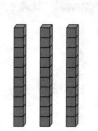

30 ones in all

Count

Count the tens. Write your answer.

1

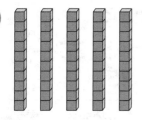

___5___ tens = ___50___ ones

3

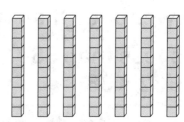

_____ tens = _____ ones

2

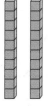

_____ tens = _____ ones

4

_____ tens = _____ ones

Comparing Numbers

You can use objects to help compare numbers.

Examples

Compare tens first.
23 has fewer tens than 47.

23 is less than 47.
23 < 47

Compare ones when tens
are the same.
32 has fewer ones than 38.

32 is less than 38
32 < 38

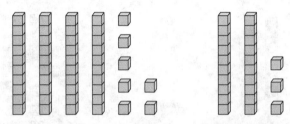

You can say it a different
way. 47 has more
tens than 23.

47 is greater than 23.
47 > 23

Sometimes numbers are
the same.

25 is equal to 25.
25 = 25

Compare

Use objects to help compare. Write **greater than, less than,** or **equal to**. Then write >, <, or =.

1 21 and 57

21 is _____less than_____ 57.

21 __<__ 57

2 43 and 26

43 is _____ 26.

43 _____ 26

Name _____

Count the ones. Write how many ones. Write how many tens.

1 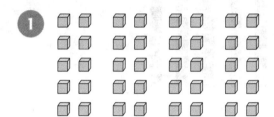   **2**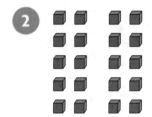

There are _____ ones.   There are _____ ones.

So there are _____ tens.   So there are _____ tens.

Use paper clips to make each number. Write the number as a ten and ones.

3 13 is _____ ten

and _____ ones.

4 17 is _____ ten

and _____ ones.

5 11 is _____ ten

and _____ one.

6 19 is _____ ten

and _____ ones.

Name _____

Count the tens. Tell how many ones. Write your answers.

7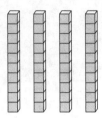

8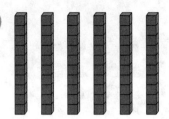

_____ tens = _____   _____ tens = _____

Use objects to help compare. Write **greater than, less than**, or **equal to**. Then write >, <, or =.

9 14 and 68

14 is _____ 68.

14 _____ 68

11 45 and 47

45 is _____ 47.

45 _____ 47

10 75 and 33

75 is _____ 33.

75 _____ 33

12 26 and 26

26 is _____ 26.

26 _____ 26

Name _____

Adding Digits

Numbers have digits.

5 This number has one digit. It shows 5 ones.

23 This number has two digits. It shows 2 tens and 3 ones.

Example

You can add digits.

```
  2 | 3
+   | 5
    | 8
```

```
  2 | 3
+   | 5
  2 | 8
```

Add the ones digits first.
3 + 5 = 8

Then write the tens digit.
2

23 + 5 = 28

Add

Write the sum.

1 12
    + 4
    16

2 34
    + 3

3 21
    + 2

4 10
    + 5

5 42
    + 6

6 13
    + 4

Show Tens and Ones

You can use objects and pictures to show numbers.

Examples

You can use cubes to show digits.

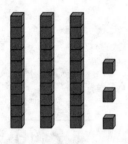

33

You can draw to show digits.

16

Count

Look at each picture. Count the tens and ones. Write the number.

1 __28__

2 _____

3 _____

4  _____

Showing Tens and Ones on a Chart

You can show numbers on a Place Value Chart.

Example

Tens	Ones
1	4

1 ten = 10   4 ones = 4

1 ten and 4 ones = 14

Count

Write how many tens. Write how many ones. Write the number.

1

Tens	Ones
2	6

The number is __26__

2

Tens	Ones
_____	_____

The number is _____

Adding Two-Digit Numbers

You can use models to add.

Example

Add 17 + 15.

Put the ones together.
7 + 5 = 12
Make 1 ten out of 10 ones.

Put the tens together.
Then add 12.

Tens	Ones

Tens	Ones

17 + 15 = 32

Add

Write the sum.

1

Tens	Ones

18 + 16 = _____

2

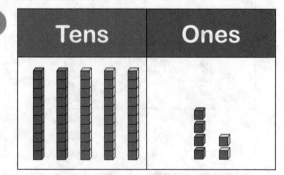

Tens	Ones

24 + 32 = _____

Name _____

Finding 10 More or 10 Less

You can show 10 more than a number. You can show 10 less than a number.

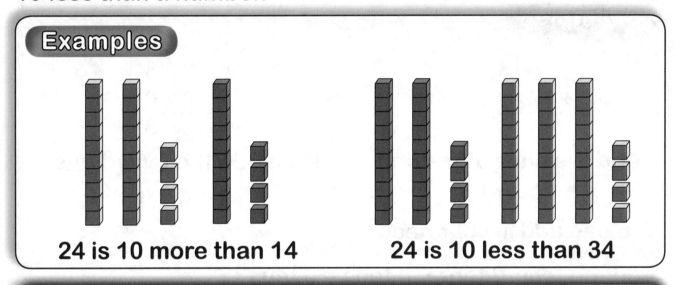

Examples

24 is 10 more than 14   24 is 10 less than 34

Solve

Find 10 more or 10 less. Write your answer.

1 42

10 more than 42 is ___52___.

10 less than 42 is ___32___.

2 29

10 more than 29 is _____.

10 less than 29 is _____.

3 36

10 more than 36 is _____.

10 less than 36 is _____.

Name _____

Adding Multiples of 10

You can add tens to a number.

Example

```
  2 │ 3              2 │ 3
+ 4 │ 0           + 4 │ 0
────┼──           ────┼──
    │ 3              6 │ 3
```

Add the ones digits first.   Then add the tens digits.

3 + 0 = 3   2 + 4 = 6

You can add in your head.

Add the tens. 2 tens + 4 tens = 6 tens

Look at the ones. The ones do not change. 3 ones

6 tens 3 ones = 63

Add

Write the sum.

1.
```
   30
+ 12
────
   42
```

2.
```
   10
+ 15
────
```

3.
```
   14
+ 40
────
```

4.
```
   23
+ 20
────
```

5.
```
   50
+ 12
────
```

6.
```
   20
+ 13
────
```

Subtract Multiples of 10

You can subtract multiples of ten.

Example

$$\begin{array}{r} 5\ |0 \\ -\ 2\ |0 \\ \hline |0 \end{array}$$

Both numbers have 0 ones.
The difference will have 0 ones.

$$\begin{array}{r} 5\ 0 \\ -\ 2\ 0 \\ \hline 3\ 0 \end{array}$$

Subtract the tens digits.
$$5 - 2 = 3$$

$$50 - 20 = 30$$

You can also subtract in your head.

Subtract the tens.

5 tens – 2 tens = 3 tens

$$50 - 20 = 30$$

Subtract

Write the difference.

1. $$\begin{array}{r} 70 \\ -\ 40 \\ \hline 30 \end{array}$$

2. $$\begin{array}{r} 40 \\ -\ 30 \\ \hline \end{array}$$

3. $$\begin{array}{r} 50 \\ -\ 20 \\ \hline \end{array}$$

4. $$\begin{array}{r} 30 \\ -\ 10 \\ \hline \end{array}$$

5. $$\begin{array}{r} 70 \\ -\ 20 \\ \hline \end{array}$$

6. $$\begin{array}{r} 90 \\ -\ 20 \\ \hline \end{array}$$

Name _____

Look at each picture. Count the tens and ones.
Write the number.

1  _____

2 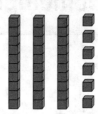 _____

Count the cubes. Write the numbers.

3

Tens	Ones
____	____

4

Tens	Ones
____	____

The number is _____   The number is _____

Add. Write the sum. Regroup if you need to.

5

Tens	Ones

32 + 25 = _____

6

Tens	Ones

27 + 16 = _____

Use objects to count. Write your answer.

7 24

10 more than 24 is _____

10 less than 24 is _____

8 81

10 more than 81 is _____

10 less than 81 is _____

Add or subtract. Write the sum or difference.

9
$$\begin{array}{r} 35 \\ +\ 4 \\ \hline \end{array}$$

10
$$\begin{array}{r} 52 \\ +\ 5 \\ \hline \end{array}$$

11
$$\begin{array}{r} 23 \\ +\ 60 \\ \hline \end{array}$$

12
$$\begin{array}{r} 36 \\ -\ 30 \\ \hline \end{array}$$

13
$$\begin{array}{r} 30 \\ -\ 20 \\ \hline \end{array}$$

14
$$\begin{array}{r} 70 \\ -\ 50 \\ \hline \end{array}$$

15
$$\begin{array}{r} 40 \\ +\ 30 \\ \hline \end{array}$$

16
$$\begin{array}{r} 28 \\ +\ 20 \\ \hline \end{array}$$

17
$$\begin{array}{r} 18 \\ +\ 50 \\ \hline \end{array}$$

Name _____

Length and Weight

You measure to find the amount or size of an object.
Length tells how long. Weight tells how heavy.

Examples

Length

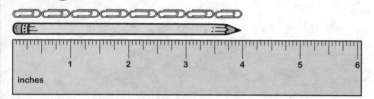

Count the paper clips. The pencil is 8 paper clips long.

The pencil is 4 inches long.

Weight

A scale can show which is heavier.

The book is heavier than the banana.

Measure

Write your answer.

 Find a pen. How long is the pen? Use paper clips.
The pen is _____ paper clips long.

Circle the object that is heavier.

Ways to Measure

You can measure the same object in different ways.

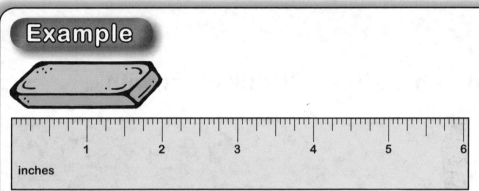

Example

The eraser is 2 inches long.

The apple is heavier than the eraser.
The eraser is lighter than the apple.

Measure

Write or draw your answers.

1 Find a spoon. How long is the spoon? Use a ruler. The spoon is _____ inches long.

2

Which object is heavier? Circle your answer.

Name _____

"More" or "Less"

Some objects hold more. Some objects hold less.

Example

Jenn fills a bowl with marbles. She fills a jar with marbles.

Which container holds more marbles? Which holds less?

Jenn thinks the jar holds more. She counts the marbles to check.

52 marbles   119 marbles

Compare

Circle the container you think holds more.

Order Three Objects by Length

You can put objects in order from longest to shortest.

Example

The red spoon is longer than the blue spoon and the yellow spoon.

The blue spoon is shorter than the red spoon and the yellow spoon.

Compare

1 Which crayon is longest? Color it blue.

2 Which crayon is shortest? Color it green.

3 Color the shortest pencil red.

4 Color the longest pencil blue. Make the other pencil orange.

Comparing Lengths of Objects

You can compare lengths of objects.

Examples

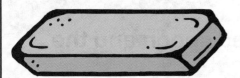

The pen is shorter than the eraser.

The pen is longer than the spoon.

Compare

Measure the objects in the picture. You can use string, paper clips, or other objects to measure. Which is longer? Circle the longer object.

1
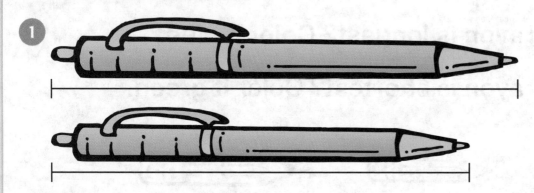

2
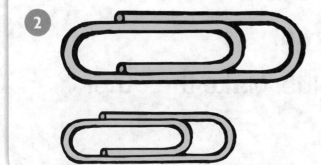

Sorting Objects

You can put matching objects into groups.
This is called sorting.

Example

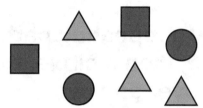

Some shapes are red. Some are blue. You can sort them into two groups by color. One group has red shapes. The other has blue shapes.

There are four red shapes.   There are three blue shapes.

Sort

Sort the shapes into two groups by color. Draw the groups in the boxes. Count the number of shapes in each box. Write the number of shapes under the box.

Group 1	Group 2

_____   _____

Name _____

Patterns

A pattern is an ordered set of numbers or objects arranged according to a rule.

Examples

These shapes follow a repeating pattern. The pattern begins with a square, then a circle, then a triangle. Then the pattern repeats over and over.

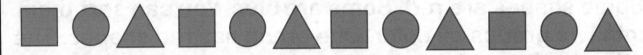

These numbers follow a repeating pattern. Each number is two more than the one before it. 1+2=3, 3+2=5, 5+2=7, and so on.

$$1, 3, 5, 7, 9, 11, 13, 15\ldots$$

Arrange

Complete the Pattern

1. ⬠ ▬) ⬠ ▬) ⬠ ___)

2. A, B, C, D, E, _____

3. 5, 10, 15, _____, 25

4. ➡ ➡ ✖ ○ ___ ➡ ✖ ○ ➡ ➡ ✖ ○

Name _____

Identifying Coins

We use many different types of coins as money. Here are the most common coins we use.

 This is a penny. A penny is worth one cent. You can write one cent as 1¢.

one penny = one cent = 1¢

 This is a nickel. A nickel is worth five cents. You can write five cents as 5¢.

one nickel = five cents = 5¢

 This is a dime. A dime is worth ten cents. You can write ten cents as 10¢.

one dime = ten cents = 10¢

 **This is a quarter.** A quarter is worth twenty-five cents. You can write twenty-five cents as 25¢.

one quarter = twenty-five cents = 25¢

Identify

Identify the Coin

    Name _____   Value _____

2   Name _____   Value _____

3   Name _____   Value _____

4   Name _____   Value _____

Time in Hours and Half-Hours

You can use a clock to tell time.

Examples

The short hand is the hour hand.
It points to the hour.

Minute
Hour

The long hand is the minute hand.

There are 60 minutes in an hour.

This clock shows 4:00.

We say "o'clock" when the minute hand points to 12.

This clock shows 9:30.

We say "30" when the minute hand is on 6.

Tell Time

Look at each clock. Write the time.

    3:30

    _____

   _____

   _____

Telling Time with Digital Clocks

A digital clock does not use minute or hour hands.
It shows time with numbers and a :

Examples

Both clocks show 4:30.

This digital clock shows three o'clock.
There are no minutes after the hour. Two zeroes
follow the :

Tell Time

Write the time in each clock.

1 two o'clock.
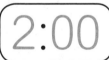
2:00

2 one thirty
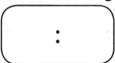
:

3 eight o'clock

:

4 seven o'clock
:

5 five thirty

:

6 three o'clock
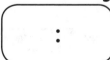
:

Name _____

Use paper clips or other objects and a ruler to measure. Write your answers.

1 Find a shoe. How long is the shoe? Use paper clips. The shoe is _____ paper clips long.

2 Use the same shoe. How long is the shoe? Use a ruler. The shoe is _____ inches long.

3 Complete this pattern:

 _____

4 Name this coin. What is the value of this coin?

   Name _____ Value _____

5 Circle the object that is heavier.

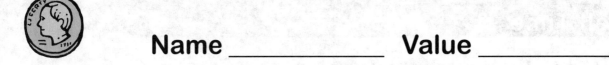

6 Which crayon is longest? Color it red.

7 Which crayon is shortest? Color it yellow.

8 **Circle the container you think holds more.**

9 **What time does the clock show? Write the time.**

_____

10 **It is nine thirty.**
Write the time in the clock.

:

11 **Sort the shapes into two groups by color.**
Draw the groups in the boxes. Count the number
of shapes in each box. Write the number under
the box.

Group 1	Group 2

_____   _____

Name _____

Names of Shapes

Shapes have names.

Examples

 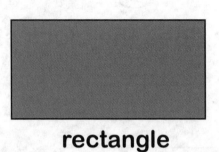 

square   triangle   rectangle   circle

Identify

Circle the name of the shape.

1

2

circle square (triangle)   rectangle circle square

3 Circle the rectangle.

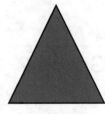  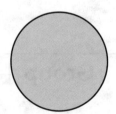

4 Color the circle green.

  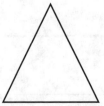

Shapes Can Be Different Colors

Shapes can be different colors. They keep their names.

Example

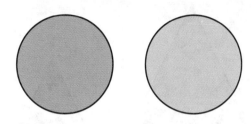

The shapes are different colors.
They are both circles.

Identify

Circle the matching shapes.

1

2

3

Name _____

Shapes and Size

Shapes can be any size. They keep their names.

Example

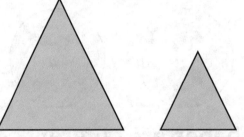

The shapes are different sizes.
They are both triangles.

Identify

Find the shape that matches. Color it blue.

1  |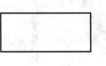

2 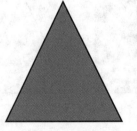 |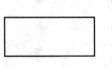

3  |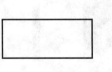

Name _____

Turned Shapes

Shapes can be turned. They still keep their names.

Example

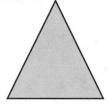 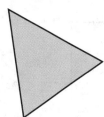 

These are all triangles.

Identify

1 **Color the rectangles.**

  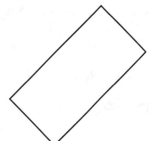 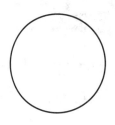

2 **Color the triangles.**

 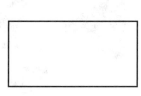 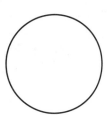 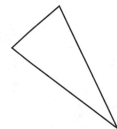

Name _____

Comparing Shapes

Shapes can be any color. Shapes can be any size.
Shapes can be turned in any way. They keep their names.

Example

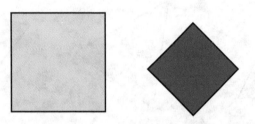

The shapes are different colors.
The shapes are different sizes.
The shapes are turned in different ways.
Both shapes are squares.

Compare

Write T on the triangles. Write S on the squares.
Write R on the rectangles.

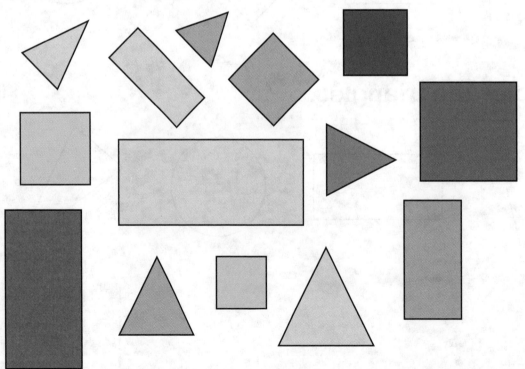

Drawing Shapes

You can draw shapes. Dot paper can make it easier.

Example

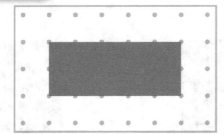 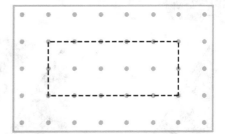

Draw another rectangle. Use the dots to
help you make it the same size.

Draw

1 Look at the blue square.
Draw a red square on the dots.
Try to make it the same size.

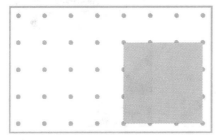 

2 Look at the blue triangle.
Draw a red triangle on the dots.
Try to make it the same size.

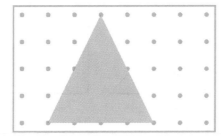 

Name _____

More Practice with Shapes

You can put shapes together to make different shapes.
You can use small shapes to make a larger shape.

Examples

There are two shapes.   Turn one. Put them together.   Now there is a new shape.

Solve

1 What set of two shapes can make this shape?
Circle the shapes.

2 What set of shapes can make this shape?
Circle the shapes.

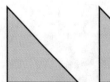
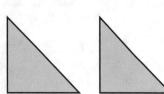

Shapes in Objects

Solid objects are not flat.
Some objects have sides that look like flat shapes.

Example Circle ➡️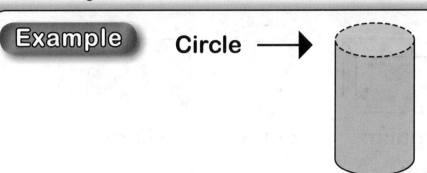

You can see a circle in this solid object.

Identify

Look at each object. What shape do you see?
Circle the name.

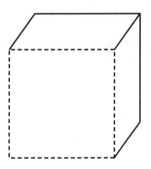

triangle   circle   square   rectangle

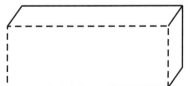

triangle   circle   square   rectangle

Solid Figures

Solid figures have length, width, and height.

Examples

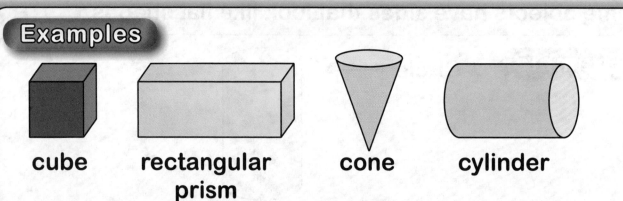

cube   rectangular   cone   cylinder
                 prism

Identify

1 Circle the cylinder.

 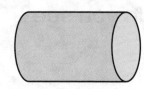

2 Color the rectangular prism green.

  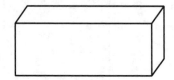

Circle the name of the solid figure. Then write the name.

3

cube   cone   cylinder

_____

4

cylinder   cube   cone

_____

Finding Solid Figures

Many objects look like solid figures.

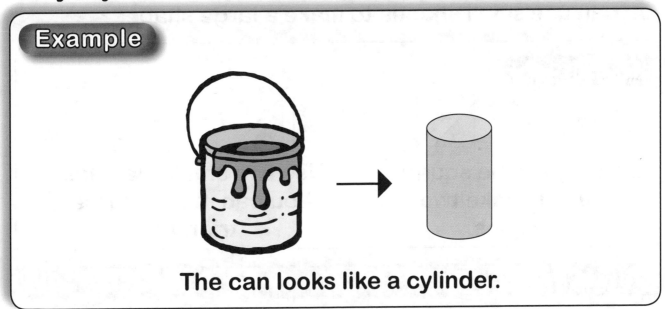

Example

The can looks like a cylinder.

Identify

Look at the solid figure.
Circle the objects that have the same shape.

Making Shapes

You can break apart large shapes to make small shapes.
You can use small shapes to make a large shape.

Examples

Break apart the square.
You can make two
triangles.

Use two small triangles.
You can make a large
triangle.

Solve

1 Draw a rectangle on your own paper. Cut it into small shapes. Ask an adult for help.
What small shapes did you make?

_____

2 Look at your small shapes. Make a large shape with them.

3 Find two cubes, such as blocks. The cubes should be the same size. Put one on top of the other.

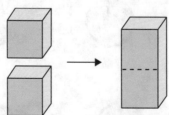

Circle the name of the new shape

cone   cylinder   rectangular prism

Name _____

Making Equal Parts

You can divide shapes into equal parts.

Examples

A shape can be divided into 2 equal parts. Each equal part is a half of the shape. This shape has 2 halves.

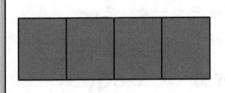

A shape can be divided into 4 equal parts. Each equal part is a fourth of the shape. Each equal part is also called a quarter. This shape has 4 quarters.

Identify

1 How many equal parts does the shape have?   _4_

Is the shape divided into halves or fourths?   _____

2 Divide the circle into halves. How many equal parts does the circle have?   _____

3 Divide the rectangle into fourths.
How many equal parts does the rectangle have?   _____

Describing Number of Equal Parts

You can describe equal parts. You can tell how many parts.

Examples

1 of 2 parts is red.

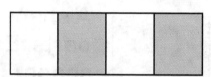

2 of 4 parts are blue.

Describe

1 Color 1 of 4 equal parts.

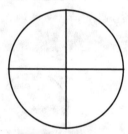

2 Color 3 of 4 equal parts.

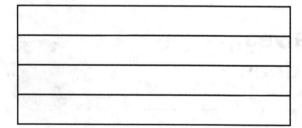

3 Color 1 of 2 equal parts.

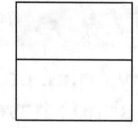

4 Color 4 of 4 equal parts.

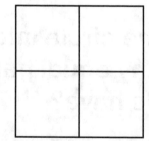

5 Look at the squares in questions 3 and 4. Which has smaller parts? Tell why.

_____

Name _____

① Circle the name of the shape.

circle   rectangle   triangle

② Circle the name of the solid figure.

cube   cone   cylinder

③ Color 3 of the 4 equal parts.

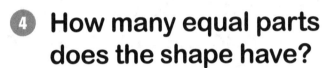

④ How many equal parts does the shape have?

_____

Is the shape divided into halves or fourths?

_____

⑤ Find the shape that matches. Circle it.

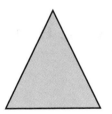   

⑥ Color the squares.

7 **What shape do you see?**
Circle the name.

rectangle   square   circle   triangle

8 **Look at the solid figure.**
Circle the object that has the same shape.

9 **Look at the two red shapes.**
What new shape can you make?
Circle the name of the new shape.

square   triangle   cone   circle

10 **Color 3 of the 4 equal parts.**   **Color 1 of the 2 equal parts.**

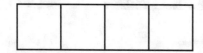   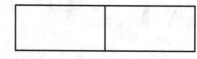

Circle the rectangle with the smaller parts.
Tell why the parts are smaller.

_____

Data

Do your friends like 🍓, 🍌, or 🫐 best?

Sarah asked her family and friends. She made a list.

The list shows data or facts.

Example

Sarah's List

🍓 Izzy, Dan, Kyle, and Anna

🍌 Dad

🫐 Mom and Tiana

Interpret

Write your answers. Use the list to help.

1 How many people like 🫐 best? ____2____ people

2 How many people like 🍓 best? _____ people

3 How many people like 🍌 best? _____ person

4 Which fruit has the most votes? Circle your answer.

🍓   🍌   🫐

5 Which fruit has the least votes? Circle your answer.

🍓   🍌   🫐

Name _____

Organizing and Representing Data

You can show data on a graph.

Example

Here is a graph. It shows Sarah's data on favorite fruits.

Favorite Fruits

The graph makes the data easy to see. There are two votes for oranges.

Graph

Here is a list. It tells which game people liked best.

Draw circles on the graph to show how each person voted.

⚽ Alex, Ana, Pam, Jin

🏀 Emma, Mai, Ted

🏈 Rico

Favorite Sport

⚽				
🏀				
🏈				

Name _____

More Practice with Data

How do children get to school?

Look at the answers 9 children gave.

You can show the answers on a graph.

Graph

Show how children get to school. Look at each child's answer.

Put a ▲ in a row to show each answer.

Kate: I take the bus.	**Josh:** I ride in a car.	**Gamal:** I ride in a car.
Dani: I walk.	**Lina:** I take the bus.	**Abay:** I take the bus.
Emily: I walk.	**Akio:** I take the bus.	**Mike:** I walk.

Ways to Get to School

How do most children get to school?

Name _____

Questions about Data

You can ask and answer questions about data.

Example

John asked some friends about which pet they like best.
John shows their answers on this graph.

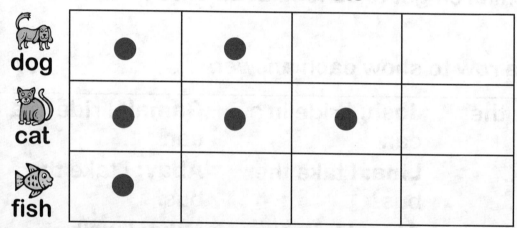

Favorite Pets

Interpret

Read the questions. Write your answers.
Use the graph to help.

1. How many people like fish the best? ____1____

2. How many people like dogs the best? _____

3. How many people like cats the best? _____

4. How many people did John ask? _____

5. How many people like cats and fish? _____

Name _____

Look at the graph. It shows the fruit that children like best.

Favorite Fruit

Read the questions. Write your answers.
Use the graph to help.

1. How many people like ⬤ best? _____

2. How many people like 🍍 best? _____

3. How many people like 🍎 best? _____

4. How many people like 🍎 and ⬤ the best? _____

5. Which fruit has the least votes? Circle your answer.

Name _____

Look at the data.

2 people like .

3 people like .

1 person likes .

6 Draw ● in the graph to show the data.

Favorite Activity

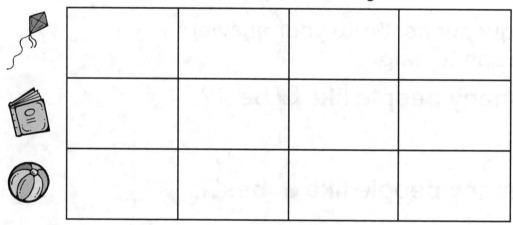

7 Look at the graph. What gets the most votes? Circle your answer.

8 Look at the graph. What is liked less than ? Circle your answer.

Tell how many. Write the number.

1 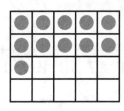 _____

2 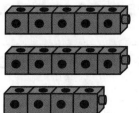 _____

Add to find how many. Use the number line to help.

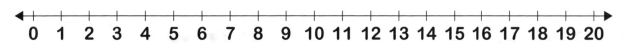

3

11 + 6 = _____ in all

4

4 + 4 = _____ in all

5 11 + 3 = _____

7 18 + 2 = _____

6 Joe has 4 .

Luis has 3 .

How many in all?

4 + 3 = _____

8 There is 1 ✈ on the chair.
There are 7 ✈ on the floor.
How many ✈ in all?

1 + 7 = _____ ✈

Name _____

Subtract. Write the difference.
Use the number line to help.

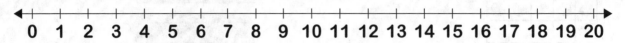

9 ⊗⊗⊗⊗⊗⊗

6 – 6 = _____

11 ☐⊠⊠⊠⊠

5 – 4 = _____

10 ☐☐☐⊠

4 – 1 = _____

12 ●●⊗

3 – 1 = _____

Subtract to find the difference.

13 17 – 17 = _____

14 5 – 0 = _____

15 9 – 1 = _____

16 7 – 6 = _____

17 12 – 9 = _____

18 19 – 17 = _____

19 15 – 8 = _____

20 11 – 9 = _____

Solve. Write the difference.

21 There are 20 🥕 in a garden.
Will pulls up 3 🥕.

How many 🥕 are left in the garden?

20 – 3 = _____ 🥕

22 Cora counted 9 🐝 in the garden.

8 🐝 flew away.

How many 🐝 are still in the garden?

9 – 8 = _____ 🐝

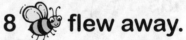

Name _____

Count by 1s, 5s, or 10s. Write the missing numbers.

23 2   3   4   ____ ____ ____ ____ ____

24 45 50   ____ ____ ____ ____ ____

25 0   10   20   ____ ____ ____ ____ ____

Look at the chart. Write an addition sentence. Then write a subtraction sentence.

26

10	
7	3

_____ + _____ = _____

_____ − _____ = _____

27

13	
4	9

_____ + _____ = _____

_____ − _____ = _____

Read the number sentences. Write the missing number.

28 3 + [?] = 14

14 − 3 = _____

3 + _____ = 14

29 6 + [?] = 19

19 − 6 = _____

6 + _____ = 19

Name _____

Count the tens. Tell how many ones. Write your answers.

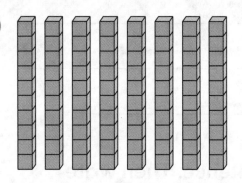
30

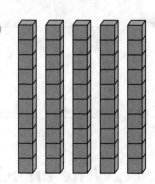
31

_____ tens = _____ ones   _____ tens = _____ ones

Use objects to help compare. Write **greater than, less than,** or **equal to.** Then write **>, <,** or **=**

32 38 and 38

38 is _____ 38.

38 _____ 38

33 12 and 21

12 is _____ 21.

12 _____ 21

Add or subtract. Write the sum or difference.

34   73
      + 4
     _____

35   80
     + 11
     _____

36   50
     − 30
     _____

Find 10 more or 10 less. Write your answer.

37 76

10 more than 76 is _____.

10 less than 76 is _____.

38 **59**

10 more than 59 is _____.

10 less than 59 is _____.

Add. Write the sum. Regroup if you need to.

39

Tens	Ones

22 + 31 = _____

40

Tens	Ones

43 + 17 = _____

41 **Circle the object that is heavier.**

42 **Name this coin. What is the value of this coin?**

Name   _____
Value   _____

Look at each clock. Write the time.

43

_____

44

_____

45 **Write the time in digital clock.**   **seven-thirty**

$$\boxed{\quad : \quad}$$

46 **Complete this pattern: 2, 4, 6, 8, 10, ____, 14, 16**

47 **Write T on the triangles. Write S on the squares.
Write R on the rectangle.**

48 **Color 3 of 4 equal parts.**

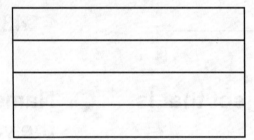

Look at the graph. Read the questions. Write your answers.

49 **How many children like dogs the best?**

_____

50 **How many more children liked fish than cats?**

_____

Favorite Pets

Add: To put groups together and tell how many in all. *(p. 16)*

●● + ○○○ = ●●○○○

2 + 3 = 5

Addends: Numbers you add. *(p. 58)*

2 + 3 = 5
↑   ↑
Addends

Circle: *(p. 92)*

Compare Lengths: To measure objects and tell which is longer. *(p. 86)*

Compare Numbers: To tell if a number is greater than (>), less than (<), or equal to (=) another number. *(p. 70)*

Compare Shapes: To tell how shapes are alike or different. *(p. 96)*

Cone: △ *(p. 100)*

Cube: ■ *(p. 100)*

Cylinder: ▭ *(p. 100)*

Data: Information you collect. *(p. 107)*

Difference: The answer to a subtraction problem. *(p. 24)*

Digital Clock: A clock that shows time with only digits. *(p. 89)*

4:30

Equal: To have the same value or amount. *(p. 64)*

Equal Parts: Parts that are the same number and size. *(p. 103)*

The square has 4 equal parts.

Equal Sign (=): A symbol that shows when numbers are equal. *(p. 64)*

3 = 2 + 1
    ↑
Equal Sign

Fourth, Fourths: Four equal parts of a whole. *(p. 103)*

The circle is divided into fourths.

Graph: A way to show data. *(p. 108)*

The farmer has 4 horses and 2 pigs.

Greater Than (>): 3 > 2

3 is greater than 2. *(p. 70)*

Half, Halves: Two equal parts of a whole. *(p. 103)*

The circles are divided in half.

Heavy, Heavier:

The ball is heavier than the mug. *(p. 82)*

Hour: 60 minutes. *(p. 88)*

Hour Hand: The short hand on a clock. *(p. 88)*

Hour Hand

Inch: A unit used to measure length. *(p. 82)*

Length: How long something is. *(p. 82)*

Less Than (<): 3 < 4

3 is less than 4. *(p. 70)*

Light, Lighter:

The can is lighter than the pail. *(p. 82)*

Longest:

The pencil is longest. *(p. 85)*

Picture Dictionary

Measure: To find the amount or size of an object. *(p. 82)*

Minute: An amount of time equal to 60 seconds. *(p. 88)*

Minute Hand: The long hand on a clock. *(p. 88)*

Minute →
Hand

Number Sentence: A way to show sums or differences. *(p. 16)*

3 + 4 = 7

8 – 6 = 2

O'Clock: What to say when a minute hand points to 12. *(p. 88)*

It is 4 o'clock.

Ones: A digit that shows how many ones are in a number. *(p. 67)*

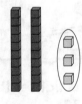

23

There are 3 ones.

Pattern: An ordered set of numbers or objects arranged according to a rule. *(p. 86)*

2, 4, 6, 8, 10...

Place Value Chart: A chart that shows how many tens and ones in a number. *(p. 75)*

Tens	Ones
2	4

Quarter: Another way to say "fourth." *(p. 103)*

One quarter is green.

Rectangle: ▬ *(p. 92)*

Rectangular Prism: 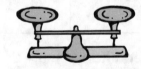 *(p. 100)*

Ruler: A tool used to measure length. *(p. 82)*

Scale: A tool used to measure weight. *(p. 82)*

Shape: ■ ▲ ● *(p. 92)*

Shortest:

The red crayon is shortest. *(p. 85)*

Solid Figure: A shape that is not flat.

   (p. 100)

Square: ■ *(p. 92)*

Sort: To put matching objects into groups. *(p. 87)*

Subtract: To take groups away and tell how many are left. *(p. 24)*

4 – 2 = 2 left over

Sum: The answer to an addition problem. *(p. 16)*

Tens: A digit that shows how many tens are in a number. *(p. 67)*

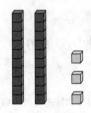

23

There are 2 tens.

Triangle: ▲ *(p. 92)*

Weight: How heavy something is. *(p. 82)*

Answer Key

Chapter 1

Chapter 1 • Lesson 1
Page 8
1. circle 3
2. circle 4
3. 5
4. 2
5. 1
6. 0
7. 4
8. 3

Chapter 1 • Lesson 2
Page 9
1. circle 7
2. circle 10
3. 8
4. 6
5. 7
6. 10
7. 9
8. 6

Chapter 1 • Lesson 3
Page 10
1. circle 12
2. circle 15
3. 12
4. 14
5. 11
6. 13
7. 15
8. 12

Chapter 1 • Lesson 4
Page 11
1. circle 16
2. circle 19
3. 17
4. 18
5. 20
6. 17
7. 16
8. 18

Chapter 1 • Lesson 5
Page 12
1. 3
2. 6
3. 16
4. 13
5. 1
6. 20
7. 14
8. 9

Chapter 1 Test
Pages 13-14
1. 4
2. 8
3. 5
4. 15
5. 11
6. 7
7. 2
8. 0
9. 14
10. 19
11. 17
12. 10
13. 9
14. 6
15. 13
16. 20
17. 3
18. 1
19. 18
20. 12

Chapter 2

Chapter 2 • Lesson 1
Page 15
1. 4
2. 5
3. 6
4. 3
5. 1
6. 6

Chapter 2 • Lesson 2
Page 16
1. 10
2. 9
3. 11
4. 12
5. 7
6. 8

Chapter 2 • Lesson 3
Page 17
1. 5
2. 9
3. 1
4. 12
5. 11
6. 7
7. 6
8. 3

Chapter 2 • Lesson 4
Page 18
1. 15
2. 19
3. 11
4. 13
5. 20
6. 12

Chapter 2 • Lesson 5
Page 19
1. 6
2. 11
3. 15
4. 2
5. 20
6. 14

Chapter 2 • Lesson 6
Page 20
1. 9
2. 6
3. 14
4. 10

Chapter 2 Test
Pages 21-22
1. 4
2. 3
3. 5
4. 11
5. 8
6. 2
7. 5
8. 12
9. 10
10. 9
11. 2
12. 9
13. 12
14. 8
15. 19
16. 13
17. 17
18. 14
19. 7
20. 12

Chapter 3

Chapter 3 • Lesson 1
Page 23
1. 2
2. 1
3. 2
4. 3
5. 3
6. 3

Chapter 3 • Lesson 2
Page 24
1. 7
2. 6
3. 2
4. 11
5. 5
6. 3
7. 5
8. 1
9. 6
10. 4

Answer Key

Chapter 3 • Lesson 3
Page 25
1. 1
2. 8
3. 0
4. 3
5. 6
6. 5
7. 2
8. 11
9. 0
10. 4

Chapter 3 • Lesson 4
Page 26
1. 10
2. 9
3. 6
4. 1
5. 4
6. 2
7. 11
8. 16
9. 12
10. 7

Chapter 3 • Lesson 5
Page 27
1. 3
2. 10
3. 13
4. 7
5. 2
6. 9
7. 12
8. 5
9. 1
10. 11
11. 0
12. 8

Chapter 3 • Lesson 6
Page 28
1. 5
2. 2

Chapter 3 Test
Pages 29-30
1. 1
2. 3
3. 2
4. 4
5. 3
6. 6
7. 8
8. 7
9. 1

10. 0
11. 5
12. 4
13. 11
14. 10
15. 8
16. 3
17. 0
18. 6
19. 5
20. 14
21. 16
22. 13
23. 8
24. 5
25. 3
26. 5

Chapter 4

Chapter 4 • Lesson 1
Page 31
1. 2, 3, 4
2. 6, 7, 8
3. 8, 9, 10
4. 16, 17, 18
5. 13, 14, 15
6. 10, 11, 12
7. 18, 19, 20
8. 11, 12, 13

Chapter 4 • Lesson 2
Page 32

0									

1	2	3	4	5	6	7	8	9	10
11	12	13	14	15	16	17	18	19	20
21	22	23	24	25	26	27	28	29	30
31	32	33	34	35	36	37	38	39	40
41	42	43	44	45	46	47	48	49	50

Chapter 4 • Lesson 3
Page 33
1. 8, 9, 10
2. 24, 25, 26
3. 2, 3, 4
4. 2, 3, 4, 5
5. 33, 34, 35, 36
6. 20, 21, 22
7. 45, 46, 47
8. 19, 20, 21
9. 25, 26, 27, 28
10. 47, 48, 49, 50

Chapter 4 Test
Pages 34-35
1. 1
2. 6
3. 10
4. 4
5. 16
6. 19
7. 8
8. 12
9.

0									

1	2	3	4	5	6	7	8	9	10
11	12	13	14	15	16	17	18	19	20
21	22	23	24	25	26	27	28	29	30
31	32	33	34	35	36	37	38	39	40
41	42	43	44	45	46	47	48	49	50

10. 2, 3, 4, 5
11. 15, 16, 17, 18
12. 36, 37, 38, 39
13. 29, 30, 31, 32
14. 41, 42, 43, 44
15. 20, 21, 22, 23
16. 8, 9, 10, 11
17. 47, 48, 49, 50
18. 7, 8, 9, 10
19. 19, 20, 21, 22
20. 30, 31, 32, 33
21. 21, 22, 23, 24
22. 42, 43, 44, 45
23. 16, 17, 18, 19
24. 47, 48, 49, 50
25. 3, 4, 5, 6

Chapter 5

Chapter 5 • Lesson 1
Page 36
1. 51, 52, 53
2. 55, 56, 57
3. 62, 63, 64
4. 71, 72, 73
5. 54, 55, 56
6. 59, 60, 61
7. 67, 68, 69
8. 73, 74, 75

Chapter 5 • Lesson 2
Page 37
1. 77, 78, 79
2. 83, 84, 85
3. 98, 99, 100
4. 79, 80, 81

5. 91, 92, 93
6. 78, 79, 80
7. 89, 90, 91
8. 95, 96, 97

Chapter 5 • Lesson 3
Page 38
1. 10, 20
2. 70, 80
3. 30, 40
4. 90, 100
5. 50, 60, 70
6. 80, 90, 100
7. 50, 70, 80
8. 30, 40, 60

Chapter 5 • Lesson 4
Page 39

1	2	3	4	5	6	7	8	9	10
11	12	13	14	15	16	17	18	19	20
21	22	23	24	25	26	27	28	29	30
31	32	33	34	35	36	37	38	39	40
41	42	43	44	45	46	47	48	49	50
51	52	53	54	55	56	57	58	59	60
61	62	63	64	65	66	67	68	69	70
71	72	73	74	75	76	77	78	79	80
81	82	83	84	85	86	87	88	89	90
91	92	93	94	95	96	97	98	99	100

Chapter 5 • Lesson 5
Page 40
1. 4, 5, 6, 9
2. 78, 80, 81, 83
3. 93, 95, 98, 99
4. 51, 53, 55, 57
5. 83, 85, 86, 88
6. 70, 71, 72, 73
7. 19, 20, 23, 25
8. 34, 35, 37, 40

Chapter 5 Test
Pages 41-42
1.

1	2	3	4	5	6	7	8	9	10
11	12	13	14	15	16	17	18	19	20
21	22	23	24	25	26	27	28	29	30
31	32	33	34	35	36	37	38	39	40
41	42	43	44	45	46	47	48	49	50
51	52	53	54	55	56	57	58	59	60
61	62	63	64	65	66	67	68	69	70
71	72	73	74	75	76	77	78	79	80
81	82	83	84	85	86	87	88	89	90
91	92	93	94	95	96	97	98	99	100

2. 55, 56, 57
3. 62, 63, 64
4. 58, 59, 60
5. 71, 72, 73
6. 73, 74, 75

7. 81, 82, 83
8. 98, 99, 100
9. 79, 80, 81
10. 89, 90, 91
11. 91, 92, 93
12. 30, 40, 50
13. 70, 80, 90
14. 50, 60, 70
15. 80, 90, 100
16. 51, 52
17. 86, 87, 88
18. 42, 44
19. 41, 42
20. 98, 99
21. 35, 37
22. 69, 70
23. 81, 83
24. 92, 93, 94
25. 18, 19

Chapter 6

Chapter 6 • Lesson 1
Page 43
1. 101, 102, 103
2. 106, 107, 108
3. 111, 112, 113
4. 112, 113, 114
5. 105, 106, 107
6. 102, 103, 104

Chapter 6 • Lesson 2
Page 44
1. 30, 40
2. 100, 110
3. 20, 30, 40, 50
4. 80, 90, 100, 110
5. 0, 10, 20, 30
6. 50, 60, 70, 80

Chapter 6 • Lesson 3
Page 45
1. 15, 20
2. 40, 45
3. 65, 70
4. 35, 40, 45, 50
5. 60, 65, 70, 75
6. 80, 85, 90, 95

Chapter 6 • Lesson 4
Page 46
1. 40, 41, 42
2. 95, 100, 105
3. 108, 109, 110
4. 35, 40, 45
5. 60, 70, 80
6. 100, 110, 120

Chapter 6 • Lesson 5
Page 47

0	5	10	15	20	25
30	35	40	45	50	55
60	65	70	75	80	85
90	95	100	105	110	115
120					

0	10	20	30	40	50
60	70	80	90	100	110
120					

Chapter 6 Test
Pages 48-49
1. 105, 106, 107
2. 108, 109, 110
3. 116, 117, 118
4. 43, 44, 45
5. 58, 59, 60
6. 69, 70, 71
7. 99, 100, 101
8. 77, 78, 79
9. 20, 30, 40
10. 100, 110, 120
11. 70, 80, 90
12. 60, 70, 80
13. 90, 100, 110
14. 40, 50, 60
15. 50, 60, 70
16. 80, 90, 100
17. 35, 40, 45
18. 20, 25, 30
19. 75, 80, 85
20. 10, 15, 20
21. 90, 95, 100
22. 45, 50, 55
23. 110, 115
24. 25, 30, 35
25.

0	5	10	15	20	25
30	35	40	45	50	55
60	65	70	75	80	85
90	95	100	105	110	115
120					

26.

0	10	20	30	40	50
60	70	80	90	100	110
120					

Answer Key

Answer Key

Chapters 1-6 Review
Pages 50-53
1. 3
2. 5
3. 7
4. 15
5. 20
6. 6
7. 4
8. 2
9. 16
10. 6
11. 5
12. 6
13. 6
14. 2
15. 3
16. 8
17. 13
18. 10
19. 11
20. 12
21. 20
22. 20
23. 5
24. 1
25. 1
26. 13
27. 7
28. 0
29. 2
30. 1
31. 8
32. 7
33. 2
34. 17
35. 8, 9, 10, 11
36. 75, 80, 90, 95
37. 30, 50, 60, 70
38. 35, 40, 45, 50
39. 9
40. 6
41. 16
42. 14

Chapter 7

Chapter 7 • Lesson 1
Page 54
1. 4, 4
2. 7, 7
3. 5
4. 6
5. 18
6. 19

Chapter 7 • Lesson 2
Page 55
1. 7, 7
2. 9, 9
3. 8, 8
4. 13, 13

Chapter 7 • Lesson 3
Page 56
1. 1, 1
2. 2, 2
3. 9, 9
4. 3, 3

Chapter 7 • Lesson 4
Page 57
1. 9
2. 11
3. 18
4. 6
5. 18
6. 6
7. 14
8. 5

Chapter 7 • Lesson 5
Page 58
1. draw 5 circles 12, 12
2. draw 7 circles 16, 16

Chapter 7 • Lesson 6
Page 59
1. $6 + 1 = 7$ and $7 - 1 = 6$
2. $8 + 9 = 17$ or $9 + 8 = 17$
   $17 - 9 = 8$ or $17 - 8 = 9$

Chapter 7 • Lesson 7
Page 60
Possible answers:
1. $10 + 5 = 15$
2. $4 + 4, 1 + 7, 2 + 6, 0 + 8$
3. $10 + 3, 12 + 1, 11 + 2,$
   $8 + 5, 7 + 6, 13 + 0$
4. $9 + 2, 10 + 1, 8 + 3,$
   $7 + 4, 11 + 0$
5. $4 + 6, 1 + 9, 2 + 8, 5 + 5, 10 + 0$
6. $3 + 2, 1 + 4$
7. $3 + 3, 1 + 5, 6 + 0$
8. $7 + 2, 6 + 3, 5 + 4, 9 + 0$

Chapter 7 • Lesson 8
Page 61
1. 9
2. 6

Chapter 7 • Lesson 9
Page 62
1. 6
2. 23
3. 103
4. 82

5. not =
6. =
7. =
8. =

Chapter 7 Test
Pages 63-64
1. 12, 12
2. 18, 18
3. 8
4. 4
5. 8
6. 13
7. 4, 4
8. 13, 13
9. Possible answers:
   $5 + 6, 4 + 7, 3 + 8,$
   $1 + 10, 11 + 0$
10. Possible answers:
    $1 + 6, 2 + 5, 7 + 0$
11. =
12. =
13. not =
14. =
15. draw 5 circles 13, 13
16. draw 6 circles 15, 15
17. 11
18. 6
19. $2 + 4 = 6$ or $4 + 2 = 6$
20. $6 - 4 = 2$ or $6 - 2 = 4$
21. 8
22. 7

Chapter 8

Chapter 8 • Lesson 1
Page 65
1. 30 ones, 3 tens
2. 50 ones, 5 tens

Chapter 8 • Lesson 2
Page 66
1. 1 ten, 5 ones
2. 1 ten, 4 ones
3. 1 ten, 8 ones
4. 1 ten, 2 ones
5. 1 ten, 6 ones
6. 1 ten, 9 ones
7. 1 ten, 7 ones
8. 1 ten, 3 ones

Chapter 8 • Lesson 3
Page 67
1. 5 tens = 50 ones
2. 2 tens = 20 ones
3. 7 tens = 70 ones
4. 4 tens = 40 ones

Chapter 8 • Lesson 4
Page 68
1. less than, <
2. greater than, >
Chapter 8 Test
Pages 69-70
1. 40 ones, 4 tens
2. 20 ones, 2 tens
3. 1 ten, 3 ones
4. 1 ten, 7 ones
5. 1 ten, 1 one
6. 1 ten, 9 ones
7. 4 tens, 40 ones
8. 6 tens, 60 ones
9. less than, <
10. greater than, >
11. less than, <
12. equal to, =

Chapter 9

Chapter 9 • Lesson 1
Page 71
1. 16
2. 37
3. 23
4. 15
5. 48
6. 17
Chapter 9 • Lesson 2
Page 72
1. 28
2. 44
3. 17
4. 42
Chapter 9 • Lesson 3
Page 73
1. 2, 6, 26
2. 5, 2, 52
Chapter 9 • Lesson 4
Page 74
1. 34
2. 56
Chapter 9 • Lesson 5
Page 75
1. 52, 32
2. 39, 19
3. 46, 26
Chapter 9 • Lesson 6
Page 76
1. 42
2. 25
3. 54
4. 43

5. 62
6. 33
Chapter 9 • Lesson 7
Page 77
1. 30
2. 10
3. 30
4. 20
5. 50
6. 70
Chapter 9 Test
Pages 78-79
1. 15
2. 36
3. 20, 7, 27
4. 40, 1, 41
5. 57
6. 43
7. 34, 14
8. 91, 71
9. 39
10. 57
11. 83
12. 6
13. 10
14. 20
15. 70
16. 48
17. 68

Chapter 10

Chapter 10 • Lesson 1
Page 80
1. Answers will vary.
2. circle the dog
3. circle the apple
Chapter 10 • Lesson 2
Page 81
1. Answers will vary.
2. circle the pineapple
Chapter 10 • Lesson 3
Page 82
1. circle the pot
2. circle the bucket
3. circle the larger bowl
4. circle the bag
Chapter 10 • Lesson 4
Page 83
1. Color last crayon in the row blue.
2. Color first crayon in the row green.
3. Color first pencil in the row red.
4. Color last pencil in the row blue. Color middle pencil orange.
Chapter 10 • Lesson 5
Page 84
1. circle the top pen
2. circle the top paperclip

Chapter 10 • Lesson 6
Page 85
1. Group 1: 3 yellow hearts, 1 yellow circle; 4 shapes
2. Group 2: 2 purple triangles, 2 purple circles; 4 shapes
Chapter 10 • Lesson 7
Page 86
1. ▬
2. F
3. 20
4. ➡
Chapter 10 • Lesson 8
Page 87
1. Dime; 10¢
2. Quarter; 25¢
3. Penny; 1¢
4. Nickel; 5¢
Chapter 10 • Lesson 9
Page 88
1. 3:30
2. 5:00
3. 2:00
4. 11:30
Chapter 10 • Lesson 10
Page 89
1. 2:00
2. 1:30
3. 8:00
4. 7:00
5. 5:30
6. 3:00
Chapter 10 Test
Pages 90-91
1. Answers will vary.
2. Answers will vary.
3. ◇
4. Dime; 10¢
5. circle the pot
6. Color last crayon in the row red.
7. Color first crayon in the row yellow.
8. circle the glass
9. 10:30
10. 9:30
11. Group 1: 1 purple triangle, 2 purple circles, 3 shapes; Group 2: 1 yellow circle, 1 yellow square, 2 shapes

Answer Key

Chapter 11 • Lesson 1
Page 92
1. circle word triangle
2. circle word circle
3. circle the yellow rectangle
4. color the first shape, the circle, green

Chapter 11 • Lesson 2
Page 93
1. circle the purple circle
2. circle the orange rectangle
3. circle the blue square

Chapter 11 • Lesson 3
Page 94
1. color the last shape in the row, the circle, blue
2. color the second shape in the row, the triangle, blue
3. color the first shape in the row, the square, blue

Chapter 11 • Lesson 4
Page 95
1.
2.
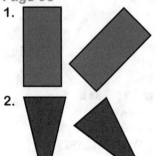

Chapter 11 • Lesson 5
Page 96
1.
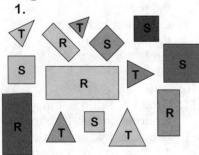

Chapter 11 • Lesson 6
Page 97
1.

2.

Chapter 11 • Lesson 7
Page 98
1.
2.

Chapter 11 • Lesson 8
Page 99
1. circle word square
2. circle word rectangle

Chapter 11 • Lesson 9
Page 100
1. circle the yellow cylinder
2. color the last shape in the row, the rectangular prism, green
3. circle word cone; write word cone
4. circle word cube; write word cube

Chapter 11 • Lesson 10
Page 101
1. circle the soup can and the jar
2. circle the road cone and the party hat
3. circle the gift box and the tissue box

Chapter 11 • Lesson 11
Page 102
1. Possible answers: triangles, rectangles, squares
2. Possible shape: triangle, rectangle, square
3. circle word rectangular prism

Chapter 11 • Lesson 12
Page 103
1. 4, fourths
2.
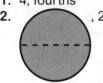
, 2
3. Possible answers:
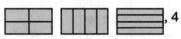
, 4

Chapter 11 • Lesson 13
Page 104
1.

2.
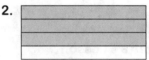
3.

4.

5. The square in question 4 has smaller parts. It is the same size as the other one, but it has more parts.

Chapter 11 Test
Pages 105-106
1. circle word rectangle
2. circle word cube
3.

4. 2, halves
5. circle the second shape, the blue triangle
6. color the second and the fourth shapes, the squares

7. circle word square
8. circle the soup can
9. circle word square
10.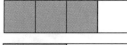
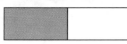

circle the shape with 4 parts

It is the same size as the other one, but it has more parts.

Chapter 12

Chapter 12 • Lesson 1
Page 107
1. 2
2. 4
3. 1
4.
5.

Chapter 12 • Lesson 2
Page 108
1.
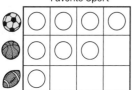
Favorite Sport

Chapter 12 • Lesson 3
Page 109
1.
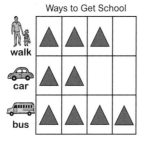
Ways to Get School

Most children take the bus.

Chapter 12 • Lesson 4
Page 110
1. 1
2. 2
3. 3
4. 6
5. 4

Chapter 12 Test
Pages 111-112
1. 4
2. 2
3. 3
4. 7
5.
6.
Favorite Activity
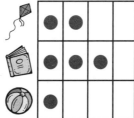
7.
8.

Chapters 1-12 Review
Pages 113-118
1. 11
2. 14
3. 17
4. 8
5. 14
6. 7
7. 20
8. 8
9. 0
10. 3
11. 1
12. 2
13. 0
14. 5
15. 8
16. 1

17. 3
18. 2
19. 7
20. 2
21. 17
22. 1
23. 5, 6, 7, 8, 9, 10
24. 55, 60, 65, 70, 75, 80
25. 30, 40, 50, 60, 70
26. 7 + 3 = 10, or 3 + 7 = 10
    10 − 3 = 7, or 10 − 7 = 3
27. 4 + 9 = 13, or 9 + 4 = 13
    13 − 4 = 9, or 13 − 9 = 4
28. 11, 11
29. 13, 13
30. 8 tens, 80 ones
31. 5 tens, 50 ones
32. equal to, =
33. less than, <
34. 77
35. 91
36. 20
37. 86, 66
38. 69, 49
39. 53
40. 60
41.
42. Nickel; 5¢
43. 11:00
44. 3:30
45. 7:30
46. 12
47.

| S | | S | R | T |

48.

49. 4
50. 1